To Lois —
Already thinking like a
meta-designer! Good luck
in your future work. With
every good wish —

Robert Farson
11/13/10

östberg™

More Praise for
The Power of Design

"This is Richard Farson's masterpiece—the one and only book that illuminates the interdependence of design, organization, and leadership."

Warren Bennis, University Professor, University of Southern California, and Author

"A provocative *tour de force* re-imaging what design could be as the tool for helping us grapple with the deeply systemic and institutional challenges in our rapidly changing world. This book is a must-read not only for designers and their students but for anyone concerned with our collective future. A stunning and powerful book!"

John Seely Brown, Former Chief Scientist of Xerox and Director of its Palo Alto Research Center, and Co-author, *The Social Life of Information*

"Please get your hands on this book. Read it and ponder it. Perhaps read it again. *The Power of Design* is simply a great work. The world needs it. Richard Farson provides a map for individual and planetary future success. He provides a new vocabulary for your internal dialogue. It is a dialogue where understanding paradoxes is more important than knowing solutions, where recognizing failure is as important as searching for and understanding success, where the situations you create with the book's guidance change you and the world. I come away from it with a great sense of urgency."

Carl N. Hodges, Chairman, The Seawater Foundation, and Director Emeritus, University of Arizona Environmental Research Laboratory

"A terrific piece of work. A truly brilliant thesis."

"As always, Richard Farson is amazing in his insights and beautiful in the challenge that he lays at our feet. Farson has been a keen observer of architects and design professionals for many years. While not trained as one of us, his ability to see past our public façade and into our soul is wonderfully displayed in *The Power of Design*. By looking at the current state of affairs, often dominated by clients, in need of enhanced collaboration, avoiding the public policy arena, Farson shines a light on the good and the troublesome aspects of the design world. While taking us to task for not stepping forward to fulfill what he sees as our potential in a world full of opportunities to apply design talent, he does not leave us without hope. Farson defines for architects and designers a new role in creating a world that supports humankind so that all people can achieve their potential. By calling on us to become more engaged leaders, working with our clients as peers to employ the full range of our professional skills, Farson charts a course to transform society's view of design. It is a powerful message that we ignore at our peril."

"For most of us, the word design conjures up thoughts of making things look good, look better, of styling, of fashion, and of gussying up the world. For Farson, it's not that at all, not looking good but being good. Design is in a two-step with innovation. Its athleticism allows it to jump out of the box, and as it looks back in, it's able to improve the world."

"This is an important and vital book, not only for the design fields but for society. ... The text works its magic without diagrams or drawings or photographs, compelling designers to ask fundamental questions about what they can do to make a better world—not a perfect world but a better world."

Robert Sommer, Distinguished Professor of Psychology Emeritus, University of California, Davis, and Author, *Personal Space*

"This may well be Farson's most important work."

Raymond M. Alden, Former President, United Telecommunications/Sprint

"It takes a noted psychologist to understand architects and designers in ways that we often don't see. Richard Farson reminds of us of the responsibility we have to the public as professionals and points out the self-defeating nature of seemingly benign activities. He also outlines his idea of metadesign, which applies design thinking to the systemic problems that face the global population, and his conviction that designers have a lot to offer a world desperately in need of vision and leadership. If you seek a book that will get you thinking in entirely new ways about what it means to be a design professional, this is it."

Thomas Fisher, Professor and Dean, College of Design, University of Minnesota, and Former Editor, *Progressive Architecture*

"Richard Farson has a wonderful way of illustrating issues that should be obvious but that are in our blind spots. Once again, he holds the mirror and shows us our society with all of its flaws and paradoxes. In this broad and penetrating view of our world, Farson correctly accuses us of designing for problems and not for prevention. His challenge to the design professions—to use the power of design as agents for social change and to recapture the essence of our vocation."

Carol Jones, Principal, Kasian Architecture Interior Design and Planning Ltd., Former President, Interior Designers of Canada, and Former President, International Interior Design Association

"I first met Richard Farson in 2004 at a Design Futures Council meeting, where we disagreed over the importance of licensing architects. It is abundantly clear in *The Power of Design* that he has not changed his mind. Nor have I. Still, we share a common goal with so many in design, a goal to unleash the power of design so that it can serve a much larger share of our society. Richard puts forward unorthodox propositions that serve that goal well by approaching an important and complex issue from new points of view."

Gordon Mills, First Vice President, President-Elect, National Council of Architectural Registration Boards

"This book has triggered in me some startling recognitions of my own, among them that there is an architecture of sleep (including the attitudes of my body and mind once I lie down), an architecture of meditation (including the ways I configure body and mind in the act), an aesthetic design of (often boring) physical fitness routines, and a more creative patterning of my daily work schedule. This list could go on and on. Metadesign! What a good idea! I wish Farson had told us about it sooner."

Michael Murphy, Founder, the Esalen Institute, and Author, *The Future of the Body* and *Golf in the Kingdom*

"This is a wake-up call by a psychologist who has connected and interacted in so many ways and for so many years with architects, designers, and other visionaries. He reminds all of us of the shortcomings and somewhat meaningless pursuits and activities of our professional societies, urging us to raise our sights to a much higher level—metadesign! Although Richard Farson is super-critical with his analyses, he presents a thoughtful and realistic process to get us on track—if we care enough to improve the conditions of the world. He calls for strong leadership in the design professions. He tells us that putting enormous energies into protecting professional turf is worthless and suggests that we put the effort into meaningful collaboration instead. He questions our fascination with awards programs that are self-serving. He urges us to be mindful of the social impact of our designs. Amen! Farson states that we 'need to redesign the design profession.' Let's do it!"

Sylvester Damianos, Architect, Sculptor, Former President,
American Institute of Architects, Former Chancellor, AIA College of Fellows,
and Former Chair, American Architectural Foundation

THE POWER OF DESIGN
A Force for Transforming Everything

THE POWER OF DESIGN
A Force for Transforming Everything

Richard Farson

Greenway Communications   östberg

ISBN: 9780978555283

Östberg Library of Design Management
Greenway Communications, LLC, a division of The Greenway Group
25 Technology Parkway South, Suite 101
Norcross, GA 30092
(800) 726-8603
www.greenway.us
Companion Web site to the book: www.greenway.us/power

First Printing
Cover design: Austin Cramer
Layout: K.Designs

Contents

Preface
My Introduction to Design

I find that people who are outside a profession, standing in the margins, often have more respect for that profession than do the members themselves. That seems to be true for me. I am absolutely in awe of the creativity and courage that designers continually demonstrate. I cannot begin to fathom where they go inside themselves to find such beautiful, imaginative, and functional designs. I so admire their ability to continually put their work and themselves on the line.

But more important, I have come to have great respect for their ability to make a better world. Indeed, I've come to think that they represent the profession with the greatest potential to rescue us from the multiple disasters we face and even move us to a new level of humanity. That is what this book is about.

One might legitimately ask what business a psychologist with no training in design has in writing such a book. In my defense, I can only say that I have been involved in the world of designers all my life and increasingly in a professional role.

Both my father and my sister were graphic designers. In their day they weren't referred to by that title, of course. They were commercial artists. (I'm sure that the role such a title implies sensitized me at a very young age to the conditions that now concern me as I observe the developments in the design professions.) After demonstrating considerable artistic talent as a young woman and spending years in training, my sister nevertheless chose marriage and motherhood over career, as did our mother, who was a teacher and pianist.

My father spent his professional life as a designer. During the depression he struggled financially. I recall one year his total income was only $1,000. But with a combination of hard work and frugality he supported his family well. To accomplish that challenging task, however, he had to work on projects that placed him in moral dilemmas.

He had once been a political cartoonist for a temperance publication and was deeply concerned about the antisocial aspects of alcohol consumption—illness, drunk driving, domestic violence. But his graphic design talent led clients to offer him jobs at which he was particularly good, and ironically, he was excellent at designing liquor and wine labels and related advertising. Without doing that work, he probably couldn't have made ends meet.

Later, as WWII approached and in a further attempt to achieve financial security, he took a position with what was then called the War Department (now Defense) making perspective drawings of coastal defense installations. But he was a vigorous opponent of our entry into that war, so once again he confronted the kind of ethical dilemma that designers continue to face. I'm sure my concerns about the commoditization of design have their roots in my awareness of his personal struggles to sometimes integrate and sometimes separate his work and his values.

To show how complex a dilemma that probably was for him, I can't help but reflect on his development from childhood. He was a remarkable child prodigy in music, art, history, in practically every area that interested him. At age 9 he composed hymns, both words and music, that were published and may still be in hymnals, for all I know. He could play just about every orchestral and band instrument. He was so precocious in drawing that at 15 he was sent from the cloistered setting of his father's religious commune to study with all the young adults at the Art Institute of Chicago. When I was learning to give intelligence tests I gave him one, and he achieved not only the highest score I ever tested but the highest score it was possible to get on that test.

But the theme that dominated his avocational life was the study of biblical history, which occupied him from his youth until he died shortly before his 90th birthday. Without academic degrees, he remained an independent scholar, taught himself Hebrew and Greek, and wrote many unpublished manuscripts on church history and other theological matters, mainly in an attempt initially to free himself and eventually others from the strictures of religious fundamentalism. In short, he was a brilliant, thoughtful, principled intellectual. So one can only imagine the problems he must have had coping with the compromises he had to make in dealing with the moral dilemmas of his professional life.

That issue remains and may even be growing in all the design professions as the members come increasingly to endorse the values of the market system. In the pages that follow, I hope to clarify those issues and show a way to emphasize the professional values, to restore design as a profession.

We psychologists traditionally study personality, intelligence, cognitive processes, and neurophysiology, all with a focus on the individual. Those of us trained in psychotherapy also initially find ourselves dealing mainly with individual cases. As one matures in the field, however, one cannot help but begin to see that individuals are members of families and work groups and ethnic clusters and peer groups that contribute significantly to their actions. And those groups are part of communities or organizations, which are part of increasingly larger systems—neighborhoods, industries, cities—each with a special culture. And those in turn are part of even larger systems that can be understood only through large-scale social and political analysis. In looking at the increasingly complicated social and political context of individual behavior, the psychologist finds it eventually tends to blur with the physical context—space planning, furnishing, transportation, greenery, housing, urban design, etc. So any psychologist seriously trying to understand behavior is naturally led to appreciate the significant contribution design makes to individual and group behavior.

My introduction to the high-powered world of design began in 1966 at the International Design Conference in Aspen (IDCA), the world's leading interdisciplinary forum for discussions of the designed environment. Through a lucky break I was able to enter at the top. A distinguished psychologist from the Menninger Clinic, Gardner Murphy, had been scheduled to talk on human potentialities, but he became ill and I was asked to replace him. My talk was well received, but the great experience for me was associating with the board members, the other speakers, and many of the attendees. All at once I was introduced into a group of the world's top designers: architects and industrial designers George Nelson, Niels Diffrient, and Eliot Noyes, graphic designers Ivan Chermayeff, Jack Roberts, and Saul Bass, photographer Henry Wolf, design writers Jane Thompson and Ralph Caplan, all icons in their fields, and all board members. And I got to know some of the other speakers—composer John Cage, industrial designer Henry Dreyfuss, architects Benjamin Thompson and Julian Beinart, and theater scholar Robert Corrigan. It was a heady time indeed for this young psychologist.

We all got along so well, they cared so much about each other, and the atmosphere was so inspiring that I became increasingly interested in the power of design. I began publishing in design journals, and because of my new friendship with Corrigan, I moved into a new job. When I met him, he was dean of the School of the Arts at New York University but soon moved west to become president of the California Institute of the Arts, the new school that Walt Disney richly endowed. He invited me to come to CalArts too, which I did, first as vice president and then founding dean of the School of Design.

That isn't as crazy as it sounds—a psychologist heading a school of design. First of all, it was a school devoted to environmental and social design. And second, I was supported by two outstanding associate deans, then young and now noted architect Craig Hodgetts and structural designer Peter Pearce, a protégé of Buckminster Fuller. Pearce designed the dome for the famous Biosphere 2 in Arizona. Together we developed a most diverse and distinguished faculty that included Victor Papanek, the industrial designer who developed all kinds of inventions to enable otherwise limited or disabled people to live fuller lives, such as a radio that could be made from a tin can for three cents, making it possible for the inhabitants of remote areas of Africa to be in touch with the world. And Sheila Levrant de Bretteville, one of the first graphic designers to turn her attention to the liberation of women. And Hans Proppe, an architect who had become an environmental psychologist and documentary filmmaker. And Edwin Schlossberg, who became famous for marrying John F. Kennedy's daughter, Caroline, but who continues to lead a most interesting career in the application of technology to social problems. And Jivan Tabibian, a political scientist and urban planner who illuminated the politics of design. We had representatives of all the major design professions as well as social scientists, ecologists, biologists, and others who could understand the deeper issues in design and move its boundaries. We were trying to direct design into more humanitarian endeavors. We still are.

I was fortunate indeed to be invited back to the IDCA as a speaker, then as program chairman, then as an elected member of the Board of Directors, on which I served for 30 years, seven as president. That experience gave me an international perspective and a sense of the importance of interdisciplinary collaboration not only among the design professions but with many other professions capable of increasing the power of design.

Those annual conferences in Aspen always involved as many speakers from other disciplines as it did leading designers. All the design professions were represented as both speakers and attendees, and the proceedings included writers, artists, musicians, civil rights leaders, social scientists, physical scientists, historians, business leaders, physicians, social critics, filmmakers, and all manner of academics and public intellectuals. Of course all of the greats in design were there: Charles and Ray Eames, Bucky Fuller, Milton Glaser, Sir Norman Foster, Kisho Kurokawa, Moshe Safdie, Adele Santos, and Frank Gehry, just to name a few. But so were Susan Sontag, Steve Jobs, Gloria Steinem, Frank Stanton, Marion Wright Edelman, Malcolm Gladwell, Michael Crichton, Jane Alexander, John Leonard, Dave Grusin, Bobby Seale. Glaser, Safdie, Santos, Gehry, Stanton, and Crichton became IDCA board members. Over the years we met with hundreds of people in that league.

Another valuable experience, perhaps the one that most motivated me to write this book, was serving on the Board of Directors of the

American Institute of Architects (AIA). Each year they elect one public director (non-architect) to serve a two-year term, and in 1999 they elected me. It was a marvelous and most enjoyable experience, and it also gave me a much better understanding of the workings of a major professional association. Many of my views about what has to happen to the profession of architecture and all the other design professions were developed from that appointment.

These experiences opened my eyes to the different ways that designers approach problems, and when I coupled my understanding of the psychology of leadership with my understanding of design, I gradually came to see that design is the approach most needed by all leaders to deal with the complexities and challenges of the future.

More recently, I have become involved with the Design Futures Council through its leader, James Cramer, formerly CEO of the AIA. I participate in various programs, lecturing to design audiences, leading workshops, consulting with design firms, and writing for its publications. That organization includes among its Senior Fellows some of the clearest thinkers and greatest innovators, and it has its finger on the pulse of the design world. My membership in the DFC has helped me see what really matters in that world.

Increasingly, what seems to matter to designers is how they might better serve business. I, of course, am supportive of that idea because business is essential for creating economic growth and with that comes many benefits, not the least of which can be a reduction in worldwide poverty. Moreover, it represents a substantial source of income and occasionally supplies clients that enable the creation of the most thrilling signature designs. Nevertheless, I have come to believe that the more challenging, more responsible, and even more lucrative work eventually will be in the public sector. A major theme of this book is how to make both happen. Over and over again we will be examining the paradoxical nature of life and consequently the need to embrace paradox as a leadership strategy. So get used to the idea of going in seemingly opposite directions at once.

Introduction
The Meta Approach in Design

When most Americans watch on television the plight of starving, diseased, and desperate slum dwellers struggling to survive on the outskirts of some new hypercity of 20 million people and realize that there are not just millions but more than a billion people in that circumstance worldwide, they can only shake their heads, feeling sad and resigned that there seems to be nothing to be done about this dreadful situation.

But I have an importantly different set of feelings. Sadness, of course, but with it I feel a mixture of hope and eagerness. Hope, because I have become aware of a profession, a force really, that could indeed make a difference, that could provide healthful environments for such victims. And I am eager to see if more of the members of that profession can recognize that potential and embrace it.

What's more, saving those slum dwellers is not the only way this group of professionals could fix our world. They could make a difference everywhere and in practically every area of public concern—health, education, criminal justice, environment, and family life as well as in fostering democracy, creativity, community, and affection. What is this profession, this force? It is a collection of professions, really, all combined under the rubric of design.

Not just architects and urban planners, but literally dozens of other design specialties cluster under that title. We all know them, and admire (or criticize) their graphic designs, special effects, landscape designs, playgrounds, buildings, interiors, telecasts, products, computer programs, video games, entertainment. Mostly they work for corporations or wealthy individuals, and too often what they do doesn't make life better but worse. They are responsible for advertising that deceives us or offers things we don't need or do us harm, buildings that are ugly, disorienting, or uncomfortable, suburbs that sprawl and have no community life, automobiles that don't just pollute our atmosphere but injure 2 million and kill 40,000 Americans a year, packaged food that makes us obese. Some designers think there may be more bad design than good, but they generally attribute that to the demands placed on them by their moneyed clients.

But I also see a positive side. I see the brilliance of their work, its amazing beauty and creativity, its range and complexity, and especially its ability not only to solve problems but to make people feel good, get along with each other, do better work, and so on. I've had a chance to get to know designers and discover their remarkable talents. What bothers me is that they are relegated or have relegated themselves only to the design of things that the market will support. And, of course, the market won't take care of those desperate slum dwellers. Nor will it reduce crime or educate our youth or make us healthier. Designers, by themselves, couldn't do all those things. Their numbers would have to be amplified by thousands of people who would help them, whom they could mobilize and train and supervise. Much could come from volunteers, but large amounts of money would have to come from taxpayers. That is an avenue that designers have been reluctant to travel. As a result, not all these desperate needs are responded to.

Of course it would take a special kind of designer, one who could rise to such occasions, to derive satisfaction from serving such needs. I would call such a design effort metadesign because it represents a step up, a transcendence of regular design, meeting a set of more fundamental problems.

My friend Tom Fisher, dean of the College of Design at the University of Minnesota and the former editor of *Progressive Architecture* magazine, responding to a talk I gave on metadesign, has added a valuable interpretation of the idea in an article he wrote for *Architectural Record* magazine. He says that metadesign can be compared to public health: "The architect/client relationship, for example, parallels the doctor/ patient relationship in medicine, in which individual needs get addressed one at a time. But medicine has also evolved another model— public health—to address the needs of large groups of people."

He calls attention to the fact that architects have long had a relationship to public health and cites the work of New York's Central Park designer Frederick Law Olmsted when he served as head of the U.S. Sanitary Commission during the Civil War. But Fisher notes that architects haven't ever adopted that as a model for practice, "and even though health, safety, and welfare stand as a central justification for our licensure, we have not seen global health as central to our profession and have generally not partnered with the institutions and agencies whose charge it is to help people in need of shelter worldwide." That would require funding by public and nonprofit organizations "to take on threats too broad in scope for the private sector to handle, such as the flooding of New Orleans, the devastation along the coastlines of the Gulf of Mexico and the Indian Ocean, and the leveling of millions of homes in northern Pakistan."

In Part One of this book, I hope to convince you that the design professions, all of them, can add a new and importantly different direction to their current orientations. Embracing metadesign should enable them to enter an era of major growth and change. I will try to spell out the implications of metadesign, showing that it could come about as a response partly to the democratization of design that has resulted from the advent of the computer and the proliferation of new design disciplines but even more from the new challenges of addressing the mounting human needs that demand design attention worldwide. I will try to impress upon you the importance of making a distinction between a business and a profession and also compare the importance of design to the importance of education. Together we will explore just what it is that makes design so powerful and universally applicable.

Part Two will attempt to lure designers into tackling some of the great institutions of our society that do not work well at this time. We will look at the general state of affairs in America as an example of the fragility of nations and then examine three institutions—criminal justice, healthcare, and education—to show how they currently fail to meet even the lowest expectation society might have for them, how they don't work the way most people think they do, and how design projects might be able to improve them greatly.

One of the important aspects of metadesign is its ability to free all of us from the strictures that we find oppressing. Design has done that in remarkable ways through the elimination of the barriers that had kept millions of disabled people imprisoned in a world to which they had no access. That design mentality can be applied to liberate the rest of our population because all of us, in one way or another, are limited by the attitudes and designs that society has imposed upon us. In Part Three, we will examine the ways that metadesign can discover and address these oppressive factors in our world.

Part Four will focus on the fact that designers, notably architects, used to enjoy a great deal more respect than they now do and will examine the activities of the professional societies in design and how their current efforts to gain respect may actually be eroding it. This is important because if design is to command major support from the public, it will have to be widely respected.

In Part Five, we will get into the subject of leadership, which is a discussion that designers have tended to avoid. But if the design professions are to play the role in society that a metadesign approach calls for, it will be important for designers to exert leadership. This section will present aspects of leadership that are paradoxical and show how it is a changing game, what designers might do to become leaders, and how designers are fundamentally, even especially, well equipped to step into leadership roles.

Part Six addresses the stubborn problem of designing education, especially if it is to prepare metadesigners with a separate curriculum, as different as public health education is from medical education. We

will not spend our time looking at specific aspects of the current educational programs, which are all often in dispute, but will look instead
at the more fundamental assumptions upon which educational designs
are based in the hope that uncovering the paradoxes in those assumptions will open the door to radical redesign.

Part Seven will survey the steps that some organizations have
already taken in the direction of metadesign and explore what further
steps we might take to realize the metadesign approach, meaning prin-
cipally how to mobilize designers to care about it and how we might
find the public funding to activate it. Finally, we will look to the future,
consider the prospect of forming an interdisciplinary forum of top
leaders to deliberate on the long-range possibilities of the design professions, and make policy recommendations to enable designers to
serve the public interest better.

Part I
The Case for Metadesign

I n this section I'm taking a look at some major but largely ignored issues that must be addressed if we are to reach the heights that are called for not only in this book but, if truth were told, also in the early, private, sometimes secret callings that brought many designers into the field. I will discuss the current situation in design as it moves increasingly toward working almost entirely with the private sector and what that might mean to the future of design and to society. I'll try to understand and appreciate the discontent some designers feel about the democratization of design but at the same time argue for its benefits. I'll ask some other fundamental questions that are seldom asked: What are the differences between being a profession and a business, and what are the serious implications of ignoring those differences? I will ask you to compare the importance of design with the importance of education. And getting right to the point of the book, I will examine just what it is that makes design so powerful that we can look to it as a possible way to a better world.

The Democratization
of Design

Many senior designers, including some of the most talented and distinguished, are discouraged by what they see happening in design today. They feel they are being bypassed and wonder if what they have to contribute matters anymore.

They feel that design no longer means what they have always regarded it to mean, that new design disciplines threaten to reshape the field in unrecognizable ways, that they are out of touch with the consciousness of the younger generation of designers, that the computer has taken over, and that design has been diluted by the ability of almost anyone to use design software to approximate the results that heretofore only professional designers might have achieved.

While I am a psychologist, not a traditional designer, I can appreciate their concern because it parallels in many ways what has happened in my field. In the past, I too have been disturbed by similar developments in psychology. But I have learned that the very factors that initially discourage us can be a source of renewed strength and the basis for a healthy reformulation of what it is we professionals can contribute. So rather than being cause for despair, these developments are an opportunity for a redefinition of design, just as I have redefined for myself what I believe to be the necessary work of psychologists.

I suggest the term *metadesign* to designate this redefinition. The prefix *meta* has several meanings, but I believe the one that fits best here is "a higher science of the same nature but dealing with more fundamental problems." In a sense, metadesign is the design of design.

Let's examine those issues that so discourage some top designers to see how these perceived problems may offer new opportunities for metadesign.

It is clear that design has indeed escaped the boundaries of the traditional design disciplines, creating many completely new but related design professions and meeting many new design challenges. This phenomenon is changing the traditional professions dramatically.

The head of a large graphic design studio recently told me that one of her biggest jobs for an entertainment industry client involved building a team of 14 designers, none of whom was a graphic designer; all were from new design disciplines.

Design has become the rubric of the future. *Design* is used now to refer to almost any planned change. Some designers believe that *design* should refer only to those disciplines that are based on a visual aesthetic. Others hold that *design* refers to a particular kind of analytic problem-solving approach. But the effort to contain its meaning is futile. The term *design* is growing in application and will be applied in many ways that will make traditional designers wince. Is military strategy design? Is seduction design? How about a musical score? Surely not, these designers feel.

It's too late. The word has already escaped. It cannot be recaptured.

Design is that kind of word. It has power. It is like *psychology* or *leadership* or *communication*, each of which has come to be regarded as relevant to almost any human situation. So it will be for *design*. The term is no longer the property of the traditional disciplines. It will inevitably be used to apply to all kinds of situations not thought of as design by traditionalists.

The escape of the term design may be salutary in the long run, even for traditionalists, because through its widespread acceptance it may raise the design consciousness and design standards of society in the way that a rising tide lifts all boats. Most design professions could use that kind of help, and the metadesigner welcomes the proliferation of the term.

Without question, new design specialties emerge at an amazing rate. In addition to the traditional professions of architecture, interior design, fashion design, urban design, landscape architecture, graphic design, industrial design, and design-oriented engineering, we see a new and varied group of professionals calling themselves designers, and quite appropriately so, in fields called production design, video design, organization design, communication design, social design, network design, software design, enterprise design, and cyberspace design, among others.

Because the metadesigner is not tied to one discipline, he or she is able to embrace these developments, very often gaining sufficient understanding of these new fields to be able to organize working ensembles of designers from several disciplines. One design discipline cannot contain the interests of most metadesigners any more than the traditional discipline of psychology can contain the interests of psychologists who have moved to a higher and broader level of professional activity, solving problems and serving populations not previously embraced. I refer to us as metapsychologists. Psychology today is as influenced by the information sciences, systems theory, and the neurosciences as it is by the research in its own discipline. Rather than being left behind by these developments, both psychologists and designers are able to capitalize on them.

Younger designers surely bring a different consciousness to their work. And not surprisingly, senior designers often have difficulty understanding them. But difficulty in understanding generational differences is hardly new. True, the old cannot enter fully into the minds of the young, and the reverse is also true. But we can, with determined effort, occasionally make that trip into another's consciousness sufficiently so that we do not feel alienated from it, and the person feels understood.

And more important, even though we cannot see the world in quite the ways that others see it, we each bring something of value to the relationship: We can see aspects of their lives and work that they do not see in the same way that each generation can bring something special to the practice of design. We certainly can see the value of decades of experience, but there is also the fact that the younger generation is well equipped to bring much that is special. Some observers, such as anthropologist Margaret Mead, believe that the contribution from the younger generation is potentially so great that we may be for the first time in history experiencing a reversal in the transmission of culture, from younger to older. So metadesigners could come from any age group. Rather than being put off by the differences, the metadesigner is challenged by them, confident that while there will be many gaps in understanding, there is still a valuable quality that he or she brings to the party. Let's call it wisdom, because wisdom, contrary to popular thought, is not confined to those of advanced age and experience.

The major technological contributor to our new design powers is the computer. It is certainly a force to be reckoned with. The activities it has made possible, such as the burgeoning practice of building information modeling and the availability of architect-designed plans ready for building, have transformed the work of designers and have empowered amateurs, who now seem to threaten the practice of designers. The computer can accomplish what was thought to be a matter of professional technique and expertise. At the same time, however, it presents professional designers with completely new ways to think about the design process, new perspectives from which to view their work, new power to tackle heretofore unapproachable design problems that by and large transcend the abilities of the amateur and keep the alert professional out front.

In addition, because metadesigners are aware of the larger social and philosophical issues of introducing technology, they have something more to offer. They recognize that the computer, for instance, is not just a tool for designers but is an autonomous, unstoppable technological force that has us virtually in its grasp. We think we invented the computer, but it has also invented us. We now pursue its potentialities with an enthusiasm bordering on mania regardless of whether or not it improves quality or productivity or creativity. Metadesigners will not need to become computer whizzes because their contribution will be at a meta level. While they must have some computer literacy, their value is in their deeper understanding of the effects of technology. It will take the wisdom and perspective of metadesigners, who appreciate how technology predictably backfires, to guide us in its use.

Senior designers wonder just what they have to contribute if indeed anyone can be a pretty good designer just by using a computer. While seasoned professionals recognize that computer-aided designs are not always as good as traditional professional design, perhaps seldom reaching the heights of elegance, humor, beauty, and creativity that they themselves occasionally could, this is small comfort when they realize that so many clerks and assistants can now accomplish, in amazingly short times, respectable design products.

The situation corresponds to one in my field. Much as most psychologists and psychiatrists may hate to admit it, almost anybody can be helpful to a troubled person. Research shows that chemists and secretaries are as good as trained professionals in counseling people with problems. They may not be as good as a few of the most experienced and creative geniuses among my professional colleagues, but they are good enough to help significantly. Indeed, based on the idea that people are pretty good for each other even if (perhaps especially if) they have suffered similar problems, a great variety of self-help organizations have developed worldwide—Alcoholics Anonymous, Parents Without Partners, and more than a thousand others. Many of these groups may be better at accomplishing positive results for their members than the profession that has been traditionally responsible for that area of treatment, mainly because the groups offer a continuing discipline rather than a relatively brief treatment.

These are hard facts for psychological professionals to swallow, and many are discouraged by them, don't even want to admit them. They make some of us wonder what we have to contribute. Most of us just hide from these facts and go about doing what we were trained to do anyway. Some of us, however, view the situation not as bad news but as good news, albeit news that requires us to rethink our roles.

Continuing the analogy between psychology and design, the painful truth is that psychologists, like designers, have had little impact on the larger global society. If we psychologists confine our work to individual psychotherapy, we can see only a very limited number of people in our professional lifetimes—a drop in the bucket compared to the world population of 6.5 billion. There are perhaps a billion or more people presenting mental health problems, and most of the rest of the population could potentially benefit from psychological assistance of some sort. We psychologists often have more to offer the healthy than the ill. But when we think in national or global terms, we can almost completely discount the impact of traditional psychology on mental health. If we collected all mental health specialists, doubled our number, and worked around the clock, our impact would still be infinitesimal. As they say, it could be rounded off.

Similarly, the effect of professional design on our world is minimal. For example, I have tried to determine the contribution of architects to our built environment and have quizzed a number of people. When I talk to architectural leaders, even former presidents of the AIA, they tell me that architects account for no more than 1 percent to 5 percent of the custom buildings even in the United States, where architects are plentiful. But other estimates are higher. My friend James Cramer, former CEO of the AIA, winces when he hears me suggest the figure to be 2 percent. He says all we have to do is drive down a main urban thoroughfare and every big building we see will have by law been designed by licensed architects. Ed Mazria's work on zero-energy buildings gives credence to Cramer's opinion. Mazria cites figures suggesting that architects design 77 percent of all nonresidential buildings along with 70 percent of all multifamily and 25 percent of all single-family construction. And he argues that it could be higher. Quite a difference. But perhaps the clearest picture is presented by a recent exhibition in the Cooper-Hewitt Museum titled Design for the Other 90%, which claims that only 10 percent of the world's population benefits from architecturally designed buildings. Suffice it to say that there exists a great unfulfilled need for design intervention. The organizers of that exhibit, which took place in 2007, mention a growing trend among designers to create affordable and socially responsible objects for the vast majority of the world's population (90 percent) not traditionally serviced by professional designers. Organized by exhibition curator Cynthia E. Smith, it focused on water, shelter, health and sanitation, education, energy, and transportation and highlighted objects developed to empower global populations surviving under the poverty level or recovering from a natural disaster. I would call that metadesign.

Both psychologists and designers, then, suffer in continuing quiet frustration from their lack of impact on the larger problems that the professions were created to address. That is why both professions should regard the democratization of their fields as good news. For the first time, we have the resources to raise the general level of both mental health and design, albeit accomplished mainly by people other than ourselves.

This good news means that as metapsychologists and metadesigners, we can contribute at a different level. We need not confine ourselves to the psychotherapy office or to the drawing board, but we can begin to think of ourselves as conductors of this new symphony of resources, as managers and leaders, as arrangers of situations in which the potential of these lay resources can be maximized. Our task is leadership.

Metadesigners at Work

W e metadesigners and metapsychologists make our contributions at a different level than the front-line practitioners in
our fields. For example, I have worked on ways of using the
mass media to exploit the fact that people are quite naturally good for
each other, of designing educational and therapeutic communities
through the use of advanced communication technologies, of organizing community mental health activities that rely on self-directed therapeutic groups, of working with organizations, not just individuals, and
of creating institutions to foster such activities. Let me take you on a
brief trip through one such adventure.

At the Western Behavioral Sciences Institute (WBSI) we conducted
a research project that gathered critical incidents from group psychotherapy—more than a thousand written descriptions of the group
members' experiences of therapeutic moments—describing the specific
actions that took place, who said what to whom, etc. We found, somewhat to our surprise, that the therapeutic event was brought about just
as often by the average group member as it was by the leader. This finding made us wonder about the possibilities of self-directed, leaderless
therapy groups. So after a cautious entry into that area, we designed a
study to compare self-directed therapy groups with leader-led groups
and found them to be virtually indistinguishable.

Nevertheless, we thought we could design ways to maximize the benefits of leaderless groups. In one of our follow-up activities, I led a weekly
group meeting videotaped in the studios of the local NBC TV station in

San Diego. After editing it each week with our WBSI Communication Director Bill McGaw, I narrated a Sunday morning television series, directed by McGaw, which presented and explained various illustrative segments of the group meeting. This program was broadcast for 13 weeks to the entire San Diego area, but we had also organized, as part of a research project, a dozen leaderless groups in the community to watch it regularly and use it as a stimulus for their own meetings. We found that broadcast to be quite helpful to those groups as well as to others that had organized spontaneously in churches, bars, and homes.

Psychologists Lawrence Solomon and Betty Berzon of our staff, who led much of this work and eventually published a book about it, arranged for a highly regarded group psychotherapist Jerry Reisel to record audiotaped suggestions for group members to improve their therapeutic experience. A typical group of strangers would come into the meeting room, turn on the tape recorder, and the recorded therapist would welcome them, introduce himself and the program, suggest that they arrange the chairs in a circle, and then he would say, "Make the circle a little smaller so you are sitting closer to each other." He would pause and return with, "I'd like you to do two things: First go around the circle and introduce yourselves by your first names. Then tell the group how you feel right now. I'll wait five minutes while you do that." Periodically, he would suggest exercises for them to go through, pausing for them to complete the exercises. Again, we found this to be a welcomed addition to the group experience, leading to our producing a series of Encountertapes, which were published by Bell & Howell and made available to a large public audience.

Later, psychology professor Irvin Yalom and his colleagues at Stanford University conducted a study evaluating 17 different approaches to group psychotherapy, including our Encountertapes facilitation of leaderless groups. He found that our approach rated first in perceived safety and third in overall effectiveness.

In the same effort to extend our therapeutic reach, I teamed with psychologist Carl Rogers of our staff (who is generally regarded as the most influential American psychologist) to lead a group over a weekend. The event was videotaped and produced a number of special moments. By editing the 16 hours of video into a 45-minute presentation, we won the Oscar that year for Best Feature Length Documentary Film. Translated into other languages, it has now been used as a training and stimulus film for probably hundreds of thousands of viewers all over the world.

I describe all this in some detail because I want to illustrate how, following one interesting bit of evidence, we were able to design a number of programs that greatly extended our therapeutic influence. Instead of our being present to witness a very limited number of therapeutic moments, we were able to make possible many thousands of them.

The same meta approach could be employed in design, and in some cases it has been, where designers orchestrate the work of others, involve laymen, and conceptualize their professional calling as reaching well beyond the traditional definition of their responsibilities. But barriers exist both in psychology and design, largely through the actions of professional societies, which have not permitted the full flowering of this way of conceiving professional action. For example, it is considered unethical for architects to sell or otherwise distribute plans for housing and other buildings via mass media or the Internet. But I do want to say that the psychological work I have been describing here involving a combination of research, application, and mass media is what I call metapsychology, and I can tell you that it is every bit as satisfying professionally as anything I ever did as a regular practicing psychologist. I think metadesigners will experience the same rewards.

Metadesign is conducted at a plane above design, starting with an appreciation and even gratitude that the worldwide level of design sensibility and product is likely to improve greatly as a result of the democratization of design. With this in mind, we try to discern what contribution one might make at the meta level.

I am an outsider, but let me take a layman's crack at that issue. My guess is that the greatest applied contribution will be in the area of social design. Designers with an appreciation for the social context in which design occurs could apply their analyses to some of the new social design territories. Problems in health, crime, education, transportation, environment, family life, and so on—the list is a long one—cry out for the kind of careful design attention that is now given mainly to products, buildings, advertising, and fashion. Increasingly, a design approach is going to be seen as appropriate to these issues because designers are problem solvers used to looking at the larger context of their designs.

It will require intensive work by metadesigners to take design into these areas. Not the least of the reasons is that these public-sector issues tend to be more in the category of complicated dilemmas or predicaments than ordinary problems. To adequately address these issues requires thinking interpretively (putting a larger frame around the issue) as well as analytically (rationally taking the situation apart and addressing it piece by piece).

Because of their greater understanding and critical powers, metadesigners are able to develop improved criteria for the evaluation of design results with respect to social, environmental, and political responsibility. Adherence as a group to such ethical criteria moves the discipline of design into full status as a profession, one that is not completely subordinate to its clientele.

These new powers in the command of metadesigners enable them to recognize that their contributions need not be limited to product but could extend to process as well, to the total system in which the product is only a part—needs assessment, development, production, marketing, etc.—increasing the value of design and of designers to business, to society, and to every organization or institution requiring design intelligence.

Let me comfort the reader by making clear that metadesigners can continue to design rich, extraordinary, monumental, signature projects, what we might call "gourmet design," a metaphor I borrow from the food industry, and do it even better. You may remember that the advent of frozen food processing led to many predictions that we would be eating what has come to be called fast food. The prognosticators were accurate on that count, as we all know, but they completely missed the prospect that alongside the development of fast food would come the astounding growth of its opposite, of gourmet cooking. Who could have guessed that the leading category of books being sold today would be gourmet cookbooks? The advent of fast food did not decrease but actually increased interest in gourmet meals.

I believe the same dynamic will apply in design, as it has in psychology. The democratization of design will lead to an increase in demand for gourmet design, for design that transcends, just as we need gourmet psychotherapy that transcends.

Transcendence is what the computer cannot yet do effectively, that is, break its own rules, which is what characterizes design genius. In fact, transcending technique is what characterizes all genius. Designers who can do only what they are trained to do are limited, as are computers for the same reason. It remains for metadesigners to innovate, to move beyond technique and expertise, to reach higher levels, to summon the courage to create, to invade new territory, as great artists and scientists and humanists always have. In that way they not only provide new models for the spread of design worldwide, but they raise our sights as a society, giving us a new vision of the possible.

The metadesign path is not a smooth one. The rewards will be almost entirely intrinsic to the work. The satisfactions are deeply personal, but they come with a full measure of anxiety, as does all work on the leading edge. And because the work is pioneering and often threatening to their more conventional colleagues, metadesigners will not enjoy the appreciation that they may be used to receiving from others.

But there is no alternative. Eventually it may be difficult for designers to make a living doing what they were trained to do. It remains for metadesigners to discover and develop new professional pathways in a never-ending process of growth and change.

Metadesigners stand at the threshold of leadership, capable of achieving a new level of influence on the nature of design and on the society it affects. They appropriately belong in high councils of corporations and government, making policy-level contributions. As our global crises mount, metadesigners may be among our most valuable leaders. But will the current orientation of design organizations permit metadesigners to exercise the wisdom necessary for the task?

In Search of Wisdom

H ave you ever noticed how rarely we see the word *wisdom* appearing in the same sentence with the word *leadership*? We often see *courage, optimism, vision, tenacity, humility, boldness,* and many others, but not *wisdom*. I decided to resolve my concern over this troubling absence by conducting a conference on the subject in our institute's online think tank, the International Leadership Forum, a global, non-partisan group of highly influential leaders. The responses were not what I expected.

I had taken for granted that wisdom was not only associated with leadership, but it was fundamental to it. What could be more important to leadership, I thought, than wisdom? Wouldn't everyone want a wise leader?

I was brought up short by a comment made almost immediately by the former president of a major telecommunications company, wondering if wisdom might actually be incompatible with the skills and attitudes necessary for leadership. As the discussion progressed, we came to see that the answer to my question was not simple. Indeed, there may be many situations in corporate leadership in which wisdom, defined as seeing the larger implications of any action, would be unwelcome. Perhaps wisdom comes entirely too close to "social responsibility."

Believing society can rely on what surely must be the fundamental wisdom possessed by CEOS, most of us seem convinced that corporate leaders and therefore their corporations can become more socially responsible. After all, it is abundantly clear that the actions of private-sector organizations have an impact on many social problems, from environmental degradation and urban sprawl to poverty and disease. We can't help but think that if we are armed with proper education and make passionate appeals to what we believe are corporations' long-term financial interests, then corporate leaders will eventually follow with socially responsible policies.

We are occasionally encouraged by corporations' seemingly wise and courageous acts, such as the development of hybrid cars giving 50 to 80 miles per gallon, only to see responsible intentions undercut by powerful market demands for more speed and acceleration. So the newer hybrids give hardly better mileage than many conventional models.

The people who run corporations simply cannot be as socially responsible as we might like them to be. They would be hopelessly distracted by having to consider constantly the larger implications of their actions on humanity. And they would be competitively crippled if they acted independently in these responsible but often costly ways.

Most of us seldom recognize, however, that corporations already perform what can be considered an equally important service to society. By creating and serving markets and thereby giving us a strong economy, they make democracy possible. Democracy simply has never existed without a market-oriented economy. As brutal and mindless as it sometimes seems, a market-driven economy does make possible what we care most about—living in democratic freedom. As Nobel economist Milton Friedman said, "The only social responsibility of business is to make a profit."

We need to remind ourselves of the important distinctions, currently blurring, between market-driven business and goal-driven professional institutions and organizations. The former responds to wants, the latter to needs. The former can be smart, clever, and strategic, but at this point it is up to the latter to be wise.

Corporate heads, of course, would be entirely capable of exhibiting wisdom, as all of us are at times, were it not for the restrictions set by the role they play as leaders of market-oriented institutions. We have to understand that their fundamental responsibility is to apply their skills and attitudes to further corporate goals.

As a consequence, we need to be able to trust our professional organizations to compensate for corporate behavior, to formulate and drive our progress toward humanitarian goals. But these organizations too are becoming market-oriented and will soon be unable to pursue those important goals. When professions try to transform themselves into commodities suitable for sale to the market, they become corrupted, as we will see in a later chapter.

The strength of a profession is its ability to say no. When it loses its power to do that, we all face trouble. Some professions are already dominated by their clientele. Design, for example, has become more of a business than a profession. If our children are going to grow up in healthy environments, if we are going to prevent communities from further erosion, and if we are going to address the misery of much of our world's population that we are now neglecting, then we desperately need architecture and design restored as goal-oriented professions.

We need to appreciate business for its contribution to democracy but recognize (as its leaders already do) business' need to be regulated by values derived from the wisdom of the professions. To accomplish that, we must strengthen our professions so that they gain a greater leadership position in our society, one that matches the power of the private sector.

Wherever we look in American society, we see institutions and systems not working. Housing inmates in giant prisons increases the frequency and severity of crime. Half of the graduates of our schools are functionally illiterate. Americans are among the least healthy in the developed world. The gap between rich and poor is appalling and getting worse. Our ability to compete in the world economy is eroding. The survival of our society is threatened by looming economic and environmental disasters.

The relevant professions offer wise answers to these problems and dilemmas, but the voices of their members cannot compete with the influence of market-oriented business interests and the demagogic actions of legislators beholden to them.

To reach the heights of progress of which we are potentially capable will require intensive collaboration among leaders from the professions, nonprofits, government, and business. If and when that happens, the quality they will need most will be wisdom.

Is Design a Profession or a Business?

The corporate chief described in the previous chapter who suggested that wisdom and leadership may be incompatible was referring to corporate leadership and to the special definition of wisdom as the ability to consider the larger implications for humanity of any decision. Clearly, leaders of highly competitive private-sector organizations who must satisfy stockholders every quarter cannot be distracted by larger social concerns.

On the other hand, when one thinks of a profession, one imagines that those who practice it would put humanitarian issues first. We seek professionals' advice because we trust that their judgment is based on that special kind of wisdom that cannot be exercised in business.

The question then arises, Is design a profession or a business? I think most designers would answer "Both" because they are not aware of the differences, let alone any ethical incompatibility between the two. Because in recent years architecture and design have become far more business than profession and because designers believe the corporate world is where their financial futures lie, they have come to share the values of that world. No longer do they expect to fulfill the social responsibilities they may once have cared most about. No longer do they offer wisdom before service.

I believe this is why they agree to design giant prisons they know will create more crime, housing developments they know will not be communities, and structures they know are not respectful of environmental concerns. Having abandoned a professional posture, they cannot decline such opportunities. But the ability to argue against or ultimately decline participation in a plan they are confident is not fully responsible is the very definition of a professional. We expect that exercise of wisdom from our physicians, lawyers, and engineers, but do corporate leaders expect it, let alone demand it, from designers?

Admittedly, to the extent that designers care about social responsibility, they try to convince private-sector leaders to care also. The fact that such an effort has proven overwhelmingly futile has not deterred them from continuing to place their confidence in the eventual raising of social consciousness in that sector. What they fail to appreciate is that economist Friedman has a point: The private sector's first responsibility is to create a healthy, vibrant economy. That is what makes democracy possible. No democracies exist without a vigorous market system. So give the private sector its due. It makes our democratic freedoms possible. But do not expect it to be socially responsible. The rare cases in which a corporation does so oblige us do not show us the future but provide the exceptions proving the rule.

The growing interest in designing with sustainability in mind and the examples we read about in which a company has launched a new "green" project has encouraged designers to believe that such social responsibility can be increasingly relied upon. But I must caution designers not to count heavily on the independent actions of corporations.

We have known about the needs for conservation and sustainability since the middle of the 20th century, and many of us have tried to spread that mentality throughout all of society, particularly business, without appreciating the particular situation in which corporations find themselves. They must compete, and they must do so based on quarterly reports of profitability. While going green can often save them money in the long run, seldom does it in the short run. When it does, of course, we will see corporations trying for those savings. But we cannot ever expect them to jeopardize their competitive positions. That is why, after 60 years or more of knowing about ecology, net energy, sustainability, and the critical need for conservation, we have made so little progress—no progress at all if you take into consideration that the global ecological situation is generally worsening. We are still playing a losing game in that area, and the future looks even more challenging.

After all these years of awareness, as of 2005 there were only 60 buildings in the world that qualified for LEED (Leadership in Energy and Environmental Design) Gold certification for sustainability. Sixty out of millions. Because of increased media attention on this issue, we are seeing more construction efforts meant to comply with sustainability criteria, and more awards are earned. But the kinds of organizations that are conforming to these criteria are those that, for one reason or another, tend to be less concerned with meeting shareholder demands. Many are nonprofits, others are government agencies, some are engineering or architectural firms that can model their practice with their own buildings, still others are utilities that are essentially monopolies, and others have built very small buildings, not larger than private homes and not requiring great financial outlays. While for-profit corporations account for a few large buildings that meet the criteria, one cannot help but notice that these organizations seem to fall into one of two categories: They are either hugely successful and affluent or they are eager to improve their sagging public relations images. That may change if this current media blitz doesn't turn out to be just a passing fashion and the sustainability mandate is adopted across the board. But my bet is that for the mass of for-profit corporations to accomplish any such socially responsible action, legislation will be required to level the playing field.

We must not be misled about what individual corporations can do. Corporations will be glad to comply if legislators or business association decisions make certain they are not at a competitive disadvantage. Remember, the market is brutal and mindless, and it demands of its players devotion to profitability. For me, the prospect of unified corporate responsibility lies in wise regulation.

Increasingly, designers are told to let the client drive their organization because clients are the source of the money. A prominent architect, the former president of a major architectural firm, writes about his impatience with the complaints of designers who say things like, "The customer just gets in the way of me doing my job." He becomes aroused by that attitude and responds, "Who does everyone think is paying the bills?" and goes on to cite examples including Mozart and Leonardo da Vinci commissioned by kings and popes. "Clients drove business then and they drive it today .... No other factor should influence the activities of an organization and every individual within it," he writes. Statements like his, which surely have face validity for businesspeople, have influenced several generations of designers who now have fully adopted the market-oriented business model for their work. This man is an architectural leader, and he is hardly alone in this view. It is shared by almost all designers, including other design leaders. He goes on to describe a relationship to clients that emphasizes trust and integrity, with which I couldn't agree more. But on the issue of service because of payment, I'm afraid he is badly mistaken.

It is a serious mistake, perhaps the main contributor to the fact that design fails to address the issues in the world that should matter most. Who is paying should be completely irrelevant to the way a designer pays attention to a client. For true professionals, giving close attention to the people they are serving, creating relationships in which clients' experiences, inclinations, and needs are explored in depth, in which their feelings and ideas are respected, is fundamental to a professional relationship, to an ethical posture ... *but not because the client is paying*. We offer our professional best and we attend carefully to the client because that is who we are serving, not because the client is the source of our income. And so we must do what is best for the client in every case, and that means we follow our professional judgment whether or not that is what the client seems to demand.

It is a further mistake to think that because the client is the one who is sending checks in response to the designer's invoices that the client is the only one paying for the design, especially paying for any compromise of one's professional judgment. The results of our designs almost always affect the public, and so the consequences of any such compromise are actually borne by the public, who must cover the costs of whatever environmental damage, social disruption, and loss of community that might eventuate. We are always working for the public whether we like it or not.

Understanding the client is an integral part of our professional service, not a commodity that can be bought. Indeed, using the payment argument as the rationale is fundamentally corrupting. The designer should be a first-rate professional no matter who is paying or even if no one is. Surely we would expect a physician or lawyer or professor to give full measure of professional attention to clients or patients or students whether or not the professional is getting paid by them. To do otherwise would convey the idea that a professional's attention can be bought and that better attention could be had if clients paid more. If the instruction given by our professional societies to designers is to attend to the client's wishes because the client is paying, it is no wonder that some designers find dealing with clients to be an unfortunate burden. We pay attention to clients because that is a key element in the design process. Nothing is more important than giving the client the full measure of our professional attention.

The worst consequence of the client-as-payer attitude is that it subordinates the designer to the client and therefore eliminates the designer's professional ability to disagree and decline. Without that ability, it is impossible to fully exercise professional judgment. Our clients need all the wisdom we can muster, and they must be able to trust us to use that wisdom on their behalf even if it may run counter to their own wishes at times.

It would be a step in the right direction if, as architect Barry Lynch points out, designers could meet clients as peers rather than vendors. The route to such a change is presented in a most helpful book, *Value Redesigned*, by Kyle Davy and Susan Harris. Of course, a professional relationship cannot be simply that of a peer because a professional always has an obligation to employ knowledge-based judgment and an ethical posture, neither of which can be compromised.

As with so many other problems, the posture I am recommending is more than difficult if it has to remain a matter of individual professional decisions by the designer. To enable designers to function as full professionals, it is necessary for our professional societies to establish this professional relationship between designer and client as not just desirable but necessary. Since the current direction taken by our professional societies is toward a business model, it may take substantial effort to convince our boards of directors that this must be the future of design. If we cannot, our professions will become ever more irrelevant and worse, ever more damaging to our society. Designers' work products account for only a small percentage of the possible design work they might be doing. If design is to live up to its potential, we need to redesign the design profession.

In thinking about the designer-client relationship, I recognize similarities to psychotherapy, where the main job is to build a relationship in which the client feels safe, understood, and accepted. My own mentor, psychologist Carl Rogers, is famous for showing that once those ingredients characterize a therapeutic relationship, the client is more likely to make better decisions. Designers could do worse than take a page out of the psychotherapist's book in the creation of their professional relationships, but then psychotherapists have a lot to learn from designers as well. If we psychologists thought more about fixing environments and situations rather than fixing people, we would surely do better.

I keep hoping designers will recognize that they cannot function as professionals as long as they are dominated by their clientele, that they will see the ethical problems of being only market-oriented, and that they will choose to return to their professional roots. I hope they will see that the opportunities to fulfill their own sense of social responsibility are much more likely to be found in the public sector. It is the public, the taxpayers, who benefit from lowered crime, better community life, less environmental degradation. The opportunity for designers to create a better world for millions of slum dwellers and others without adequate living circumstances is a public concern. Because they design situations, experiences, and relationships, architects and designers may be better able than any other professional to reduce the indices of despair: crime, illness, school failure, addiction, domestic violence, and the like. That is public business.

We need the wisdom, ideas, and programs of designers not just to overcome the bad but also to make possible the good. Designers can foster creativity, community, security, effectiveness, understanding, and affection. Other professions such as medicine and education do not hold the promise of design, yet they are taxpayer-funded annually in the hundreds of billions. Their planning is in the trillions. That should be the future of design.

Is Design as Important as Education?

The more I learn about design, the more respect I have for its potential. Now when I ask myself, Is design as important to our success as a society as education or medicine? my answer is emphatically, yes.

This is not just because K-12 education is so riddled with problems that it is rendered sadly ineffective. (After 13 years of full-time schooling, graduates of the American public educational system are barely literate, the average high school graduate not having read a book in the previous year. Seniors at Ivy League colleges recently received an average grade of 53 out of 100 on what would be about a 7th grade multiple-choice history and general information exam. I hasten to add that this is not new and not a reason to disparage the current generation, which does about at well as those that came before it.)

Nor is it because the corrupt political and financial practices of medicine have contributed to our being an overly drugged nation with one of the poorest health records in the developed world. (We rank second worst in infant mortality.) No, I'm referring to the potential of design even compared to the higher callings and occasional successes of the professions of education and medicine.

I mention those professions because they are deemed so important to our society that we see fit to subsidize their efforts to the extent of hundreds of billions of dollars annually. I could have mentioned other professional areas that are similarly subsidized—law enforcement and the military, for example, but I won't get started on the inadequacies of those financial sinks. The point is, some professions are considered so essential to our progress as a civilization that we collectively support them with taxpayer money.

As currently practiced, architecture and design are not essential because they are more business than profession, often elite services, in fact. I refer rather to the potential for serving the public good. The world surely needs better shelter, better work environments, and better communities, but designers are frozen in place because there is no way for the needy to pay.

I believe design has more to contribute than other professions. Architects can make it possible for children to grow up in bright, airy spaces with decent views, a factor that is shown to lead to higher achievement. Similarly, urban planners can contribute to public health by reducing pollution and building close-knit communities. Interior designers can create spaces in which workers will be more productive and innovative and families happier. As I have pointed out, designers could eventually reduce perhaps all of those aspects of our lives that are most troubling: crime, addiction, divorce, physical and mental illness, alcoholism, child abuse, and suicide. The reason other professions cannot make that claim is that the design of environments, situations, and experiences is more powerful in eliciting our best than are the practices of any other profession. That's why design should be supported as essential to the public good. It can indeed build a better world.

To serve the public good, however, a metaprofessional approach to design is vital—working toward the professional goals that brought most designers into the field but at a higher level and in a leadership role. Collaborating with other design and social science professions, using mass production and mass media, tapping resources in the general population for help in solving its problems, elevating practice to the design of design, transforming the designer into orchestrating the talents of others—as metadesigners, great achievements would be possible.

I now think that design should be publicly supported in the same way education and medicine are. Our professional strategies should include making a case for major public funding to the tune of trillions of dollars over time. Our professional planning and lobbying efforts should seek funding at a scale that would make our current efforts to get occasional hospital or prison construction money seem paltry.

Most people do not yet appreciate the importance of design. How could they? All they are made aware of is what awards are given, usually for projects having nothing to do with how most people live. Or they see movies in which the architect always gets the girl. We have a real education job to do, and our current efforts are way off the mark.

The significant barriers to this may not be just the self-concepts of some designers as lone heroes right out of Ayn Rand's *Fountainhead* but rather the conservative politics of many leaders of design firms, who in their adopted role as business executives have probably come to share the predominant views of business leaders—smaller government, free market economy, increased privatization, reliance on the private sector, unburdening taxpayers, and trickle-down economics. Moreover, we don't have the luxury of public demand that forced the development of such programs as public education and Medicare, sometimes over the objections of the professions involved—at least not until we argue the case that design can make a comparable level of contribution to the public good.

But first we have to make that case to ourselves. We have to realize that the money saved through reduced crime, illness, and the other plagues of contemporary society would be far greater than the public expenditures required to rectify these ills through good design.

But can we avoid the bureaucracy, inefficiency, and corruption that sometimes characterizes large-scale professional activities? I have some ideas along those lines, but let's cross that bridge when we come to it—after our first trillion dollars in public support.

The Power of Form

Have you ever noticed the difference between a meeting held at a rectangular table and one held at a round table? The time spent, the agenda, and the participants may be exactly the same, but the meetings are completely different. The discussion at the round table is more informal, the leadership is shared, the communication more personal.

Making further changes in the physical design of the meeting amplify the effect. Eliminating the table entirely and sitting in a circle, removing jackets and neckties—or to promote a decidedly relaxed discussion, removing shoes and sitting on the floor—all predictably shift the conversation in directions that are increasingly open and comfortable, with participation more evenly distributed. To produce these behaviors, nothing need change but the design of the physical situation.

Design may soon become the byword of leadership and management. Because of the growing recognition of design's power to affect human behavior, increasing numbers of organization specialists think executives should adopt a design perspective. Management guru Tom Peters says it flatly: "Everything is design."

Why would he make such an all-encompassing statement? To get the answer, we need only turn to the definitions of design given us by the noted graphic designer Milton Glaser:

"One definition is that design is the intervention in the flow of events to produce a desired effect. Another is that design is the introduction of intention in human affairs. A third rather elegant description is that design moves things from an existing condition to a preferred one. This last one reduces the complexity of the idea, but I like all three definitions. Design doesn't have to have a visual component. Ultimately, anything purposeful can be called an act of design."

But if design is everything, how can it be something special, focused, and usable for leaders? To clarify this we need one more definition: Design is the creation of form. Everything that a leader deals with has form—buildings, offices, meetings, correspondence, speeches, conversations, interviews, networks, schedules, reports, communications, products, relationships, procedures, workflow, ground rules, and systems. Steve Jobs of Apple calls design "the fundamental soul of a man-made creation."

Why is form so important? The short answer: In human affairs, form rules. For example, form always wins over content. How you say something dominates what you say. A written message carries more weight than a spoken one, a printed one weightier than one that is typed, which is weightier than one handwritten, even though all the words may be identical. These are metamessages, sent by the form of the message, and they are powerful.

A clear example of the victory of form over content is seen in education. As effective as our schooling may have seemed at the time, we all tend to forget what was in the curriculum. Tried solving a square root problem recently? We once could. We just forget. But as the late social critic Ivan Illich pointed out long ago, we never forget the lessons we learned from the form of education. We learned to raise our hands, obey adult authority, stand in line, take turns, not talk about certain subjects, and many other lessons now indelibly ingrained. Those lessons are not in the curriculum. The form, the ritual, the social design of the classroom teaches them.

Designers, in particular, should have no difficulty understanding this concept because it is the basis for much of their work. Corporate identity programs, for instance, are a triumph of form over content.

Everything from the building architecture to the furnishings to the graphics of the annual report to having a receptionist with a British accent is an effort to shape the way form communicates.

Recognizing the importance of form, marketing departments spend a lot of time on product packaging, often sending a deceptive metamessage that bears little relationship to what is in the package. A box can be made to seem as if it holds more product than it actually does. That sort of practice corrupts the concept of design and denies its fundamental lessons. Indeed, the most important reason to focus on form is to bring it in line with content so that the metamessage does not undermine the message but supports it so that the design of the project is congruent with the goals of the project. Too often, of course, the goal is to deceive. We examine the consequences of that later.

Design achieves its power because it can create situations, and a situation is more determining of what people will do than personality, character, habit, genetics, unconscious motives, or any other aspect of our individual makeup. This is perhaps the most important but least understood and appreciated aspect of psychology and design. I should repeat it over and over. Here is a way to remember it: *Nobody smokes in church, no matter how addicted.*

Design has always had great influence on personal experience and the course of human affairs. We all recognize the inspiration that comes from the architecture of a great cathedral. Stage sets and costume designs enrich the drama of theater. Industrial design of accessories and tools augments our powers and makes our lives safer and more comfortable. Interior design can provide settings to improve sociability. Landscaped greenbelts contribute to the civility of neighborhoods. Graphic design can shape our thinking and motivate our behavior.

Because it is so powerful, design also has a dark underside. If mindlessly conceived or corrupted, design can produce depressing consequences. The design of cities that plan giant shopping centers can erode traditional communities by forcing neighborhood businesses to close. Massive highway construction can divide and rupture a neighborhood. Kafkaesque office designs of row after row of monitored employees or maze-like cubicles can dehumanize. Graphic designs in advertising and commerce can be dangerously misleading, promoting unhealthy products, misinforming voters, or steering us down dangerous paths. Designers often recognize this, but because they are in business they don't know what to do about it.

Sometimes, however, we are completely unaware of the subtle effects of form and don't appreciate the role design might have played in an unfortunate turn of history. So let's look at such an example of design gone wrong, for example how it helped get the United States into its disastrous war in Iraq. What? Design might have played a role in that decision? Indeed, and examining that role may help open up similar major public events to scrutiny and positive action by the design community and perhaps eventually by society generally.

While the media are often faulted in the run up to the war for not being sufficiently investigative or challenging, I suggest there is another fault, one that can be attributed to design, and that is the form of the media messages. From the beginning of President George W. Bush's call to war, the media inadvertently reinforced his objectives, helped foment a war fever, and contributed to gross misunderstandings that led the American people to back an invasion and occupation.

I refer not just to broadcast journalism's recent shift in emphasis from news to entertainment and the obvious appeal of high ratings that war stories bring. Nor to the consistent drumbeat to the war given by the Fox Network. A more pervasive and insidious aspect of the media coverage of the lead up to the Iraq war is less well understood—the domination of form over content.

As we have seen, in the psychology of communication, form usually wins over content. It is the form the media takes that unintentionally contributed to our entry into the war. That consequence has been accomplished in three principal ways: repetition, graphic design, and rules of coverage.

When we repeat a message often enough, the repetition itself becomes more influential in gaining acceptance of the message than does its content. Take, for example, the reporting of statements by

President Bush on his intentions to disarm Iraq of its weapons of mass destruction and remove the tyrant Saddam Hussein from power. With almost no variation, that one-line message was repeated as front-page news practically every day from August 2002 to end of regular combat in May 2003 and in similar form into the occupation, even beyond Hussein's capture in December 2003. Granted, there is some obligation to report the words of the president, but to repeat that message over and over again as if it were news and as if the statement were based on fact was clearly both powerful and irresponsible.

Consider the paradox of the 24-hour radio and television news format. Instead of using that time for in-depth analysis, which one might reasonably expect, reporting is often more superficial than that of half-hour network news shows. The round-the-clock format essentially repeats only the headlines over and over. Constant repetition of quotes suggesting the possible connection between Iraq and the Sept. 11 attacks on the United States, for example, when most journalists suspected there was no evidence of such a connection, eventually led 45 percent of Americans to believe that Hussein was behind that horrible act. Small wonder they supported invasion.

Graphic designs introducing the network and cable TV coverage with dramatic slogans made into eye-catching logos served to validate and legitimize the war. The presentation of catchy phrases such as "Showdown with Saddam" incorporated into striking logos gave the prospective war not only appeal but also legitimacy. Just as a printed message is usually weightier than a spoken one, a logo communicates solidity, reality, and in this case, inevitability—all combining unconsciously to convey a kind of tacit acceptance, even approval.

Design policies governing what kinds of stories and photos can be presented are again illustrative of the power of form in making the war palatable and acceptable. Rules of form essentially prohibit reporting civilian deaths or showing maimed victims or dead bodies. In one sense these are understandable policies because showing the true horrors of war can be sickening. But the effect of leaving out that dimension is to sanitize war, again contributing to its acceptability. Professional judgment in the design of such presentations is called for and cannot be based only on the commercial interests of what might increase or reduce sales.

Also at fault was journalism's requirement for "balanced" reporting. This design constraint required that every investigative report include an opposing view even if that view had little or no substance, which continually led journalists to include alongside any deep analysis the administration's unsupported statements in a pro forma attempt at supposed balance.

The first casualty of war is truth. But long before the beginning of the war, truth became lost in the overwhelming power of the form, of the design, if you will, in which it was buried.

Part II
Looking at the Big Picture

For designers to react competently to these larger challenges, to function as metadesigners, to recognize what really needs to be designed (actually, just about everything), they need to have a grasp of the larger context of their designs and in particular a more accurate picture of the situation to be designed or redesigned. Architect and graphic designer Richard Saul Wurman has devoted his career to showing how things work in contrast to how we think they do. He continually looks at the systems in which design challenges are embedded and argues that understanding must always precede design.

It is with that in mind that I will take a rather broad look at our society so that we can come to grips with some of the most difficult concepts to get our minds around, including, believe it or not, the fragility of our nation. And then we will examine three specific areas in more detail to show just how serious the situation is, how these institutions don't work the way we have been led to believe they do. But the good news is that there are promising design approaches toward correcting the fundamental problems, some that will even add new hope for better lives.

The Metadesign Challenge
for America

M ost Americans enjoy a relatively comfortable and sometimes splendid way of life. Yet under the surface, enormous problems threaten us all.

More than 2 million citizens are in prison, a higher percentage than in any other country and most for non-violent offenses. Instead of these prisoners being rehabilitated, their incarceration prepares them to commit more serious crimes.

Nearly 50 million Americans do not have health insurance, and many millions more have inadequate coverage, one of the many consequences of unenlightened policies and practices that have made us a nation of relatively unhealthy people.

Half of our high school graduates can't read well, and most of the rest don't read. This is to say nothing of the failures of education to provide genuine understanding of society, government, science, art, or to develop critical thinking and wisdom.

The list goes on: backfiring responses to terrorism, immigration troubles, ethnic conflicts, security mistakes, soaring debts, alienation from the world community, corporate ethical abuses, death penalty questions, unaffordable housing, increasing distance between rich and poor, resource depletion, environmental pollution, racial discrimination, urban sprawl, abortion controversy, gun violence, family breakup, concentration of media power, homelessness.

In some instances, solutions to these problems exist but are not employed. In others, workable ideas still need to be generated. Whether there is a need to find ways to implement existing ideas or generate new ones, the answer will always lie in fostering improved thinking toward realistic action.

Why are available solutions not implemented? The policies that block solutions and aggravate these dangers come from several sources. Some reflect political shifts; others reflect an ignorance of the scientific, professional, or design contributions that can be made toward their solution. Some come from partisan gridlock, a seemingly permanent inability for legislators to set aside party loyalty to achieve higher-order goals. All are worsened by the lack of information and opportunities for deliberation and consensus building among the citizens in whom our democracy has invested the ultimate political power.

For a society to prosper both technologically and in terms of the quality of our lives, we must think differently than ever before. Ideas, not technology, founded America and changed the world. What prevents us now from generating the sound, creative, critical thinking so needed today? What limits the thoughts and the influence of the sources we usually look to—government, professional societies, universities, think tanks? Let's take a look.

Government. The limitations of government to address these challenges thoughtfully are well documented. Members of both the legislative and executive branches are heavily beholden to special interest groups and financial backers, and because of frequent election cycles their major focus is on relatively short-term goals. The excessive influence of lobbyists and big business has led novelist and historian Gore Vidal to refer to the United States as the world's most corrupt democracy. That may be an exaggeration, but the American people are now awakened to the fact that politicians and bureaucrats tend to lag substantially behind the public in their willingness to address these issues.

Professional societies. Perhaps the most pernicious problem with professional groups is their outdated strategy of protectionism, continually struggling to keep others from encroaching on their turf. This overriding concern for protection rather than collaboration prevents them from casting a larger vision for the professions, thereby lessening their viability and their value to society. Pursuing such interests has led to their weakening. For example, only 26 percent of physicians now belong to the American Medical Association.

Universities. Because they cannot risk impermanence and the consequent inability to honor their degrees and tenure commitments, universities tend to be cautious organizations, encouraging manageable, mainstream studies rather than groundbreaking research. Moreover, they are structured along traditional disciplinary lines that discourage the formation of genuine interdisciplinary communities of scholars. It is no accident that the great creative achievements of history, those that have shaped our civilization, have been made by individuals working outside the university, either alone or in small, independent institutes. Think of Einstein, Gandhi, Mendel, Darwin, of Freud's Vienna Institute, Edison's lab, or the Bauhaus.

Think tanks. The dozens of think tanks that exist in the United States and abroad also are limited in their ability to address these challenges. The largest and most prominent are market-driven, brains-for-hire organizations that study only those issues for which there is a paying customer, who, of course, defines the problem. The rest, for the most part, are ideologically narrow, politically partisan, their recommendations deriving not from unbiased, comprehensive analyses but from conservative or liberal political philosophies.

So the lesson we must learn is that we cannot leave these troubles to someone else. Designers, the group best able to deal with them, must step up. To do that we need to face some unpleasant realities.

Just as when the sun, moon, and Earth are in line, causing a solar eclipse, we now have an unprecedented alignment of dangerous social conditions that could bring about a different kind of darkening, one that could send America, even at the height of its power, into eclipse.

An alarming thought but not impossible, and I suspect more likely every day. To understand why that might happen, we first must appreciate a fundamental paradox in human affairs. We tend to believe that individuals are fragile and nations are strong, but just the opposite is true. Individuals are almost indestructible, but nations are highly fragile.

It's natural for us to feel that individuals need protection and nations or organizations can absorb all manner of abuse, but the evidence is in the other direction. Consider how difficult it is to damage a person's psyche yet how easy it is to damage a relationship or an organization. Individuals are extremely resilient. It is not difficult to hurt people's feelings but very hard to injure them permanently in any social or psychological way. On the other hand, it is common for a relationship to fail permanently as a result of one wrong word. It takes very little to destroy an organization, and indeed, the vast majority of new organizations do end abruptly, often on the trauma that comes from failed relationships.

Nations can and often do collapse, even without physical violence. Not all that long ago we saw the other superpower, the powerful U.S.S.R., fall apart almost overnight. No one predicted that calamitous downfall. It has happened to many other nations in the past few decades.

Nations exist on land, but their land is not what makes them nations. They are built on relationships, on trust and confidence in human systems. Relationships and those human inventions that are constructed on them such as professions, organizations, corporations, government and nations are always in a somewhat precarious state, even though it may not seem that way.

The Census Bureau reports that half of all marriages end in divorce, and although some studies show a recent decline, the bureau expects that percentage to hold. According to *BusinessWeek* magazine, at least 64.2 percent of businesses fail within the first 10 years. In both cases, failures in communication are often cited as causal.

As our second president, John Adams, warned, "Even mighty states and kingdoms are not exempted .... When they have reached the summit of grandeur, some minute and unsuspected cause commonly affects their ruin, and the empire of the world is transferred to some other place."

When the public is anxious and frightened, especially about a vague but horrifying threat, they sacrifice their better instincts for the comfort of authoritarian leadership and the illusion of safety, making the step to totalitarianism a short one.

Whatever this lineup of hazardous situations might bring, it is worth reminding ourselves that democracy, even nationhood, is a delicate condition that needs our constant vigilance, protection, and loving attention. It very definitely needs the attention of our designers. Then perhaps the frightening prospect of this developing eclipse may not be total.

While I'm confident that design plays a role in all of these developing conditions, I would like to focus in more detail on three professions that seem to get plenty of attention but ironically are not well understood. I include them because they represent areas not only in which we have placed unwarranted confidence but in which design can clearly make a major difference. They form three important legs of our national infrastructure.

We hear a lot about the need to rebuild our physical infrastructure—our eroding school buildings, highways, bridges, government buildings—but even more important is the need to rebuild our social infrastructure. We can avoid the frightening scenario of a national eclipse only if designers come to see that their role is not cosmetic but fundamental to our national survival.

The basic institutions in America are all in some measure of trouble. Some are far worse than others, but none are working as they must if we are to survive as a democracy. If we lose investigative journalism, for example, which is rapidly disappearing as newspapers cut back or go out of business, we lose our most important protection from tyranny and other threats to our democracy. Indeed, the vulnerability of all our institutions represents a threat that is more dangerous because it is largely invisible. Americans, by and large, think these institutions are working well. How wrong we are.

To make this point, I will present only three of the most important professional institutions—criminal justice, education, and healthcare—but the analysis could extend to practically all the institutions we consider to be our infrastructure. And as we will see throughout this book, the professions of design are equally vulnerable. But let's see how designers might strengthen these three areas that desperately need their help.

Metadesign and
Criminal Justice

America is one of the most violent and crime-ridden nations in the world. We incarcerate a larger percentage of our population than any other, and we are one of only four fully developed nations that still employs the death penalty (along with Japan, Singapore, and Taiwan). Yet the subject of criminal justice is very poorly understood, and opportunities for the intervention of a design mentality to deal with some of the problems and dilemmas are great indeed. Like all institutions, criminal justice is riddled with paradoxes.

To gain perspective on the crime picture in America, let's look at some of the paradoxes—facts about crime that seem absurd but are nevertheless true. Consider, for example, the paradox that even if all the prisons were emptied and the inmates were turned loose we might not notice much increase in crime. This is because the vast majority of criminals are already at large, even many of the most dangerous ones.

Most crimes, even serious ones, are not even reported, and of those reported only a very small percentage are solved. Only one in four murders leads to a murder conviction. One in 20 gangland killings. Possibly only one in 10 rapes is even reported. One in 150 burglaries results in arrest and conviction. And although roughly half of the people in prison are there for drug-related crimes, marijuana remains the United States' leading cash crop. The statistics for other unsolved lesser crimes are similarly dramatic. Once arrested, not all suspects are convicted.

Many of those convicted are not incarcerated, and within a few years almost all of those who are incarcerated for serious crimes are set free. America's criminals are already among us and always have been.

Even though America has far more violent crime than any other developed country, the vast majority of Americans have never witnessed a violent crime, let alone been the victim of one. For almost all of us (with notable and painful exceptions) crime is mainly an event on television. Our contact with crime is virtual, not real.

Paradoxically, thanks to shallow media coverage and exploitative politicians, our fear of crime increases while crime itself may decrease. Thanks to Berkeley law professor Franklin Zimring's book The Great American Crime Decline, we can see the difference between the popular perception that we were experiencing an epidemic of crime in the 1990s and the truth that crime rates actually decreased by 40 percent, a reduction that has remained in place since 2000. This decrease, by the way, has nothing to do with draconian measures such as the "three strikes" laws.

But it may not be the actual crime rate that makes us vulnerable to social unrest if the actual decline is not matched by a comparable decline in fear. The unwarranted nervousness about super-predators of the 1990s continues to a great extent. That is probably due to the media's failure to present the total picture. Fear, unfortunately, is good for ratings. For example, the National Center for Missing & Exploited Children regularly reports the Department of Justice statistic that about 800,000 children are missing every year. I visited the Center's fundraising booth at my local supermarket. It featured in large letters the slogan "Every 37 seconds a child is missing." Without clarification, it would be easy for any onlooker to assume that those children had been kidnapped. The actual number of kidnappings in which a child is abducted by a stranger and held overnight 50 miles away is about 100 a year. As a result of such undisciplined media coverage and fundraising efforts, American parents have become so frightened that they don't permit their children to speak to strangers. Sadly, for the first time in our history, no adult will dare approach a child even to speak, let alone button a jacket, tie a shoe, or push a swing. We will look at that situation in a later chapter, but suffice it to say that it destroys an element of community that we have always relied upon, and community is our most important protection against all manner of threats.

Crime in America is full of such paradoxes. For example, absurd as it sounds, crime derives less from what we consider bad about our society than what we consider good. Forget about violence on television or pornography or faulty parenting. Even the blights of poverty and racism are not sufficient to explain it. Countries with poverty and racism far worse than ours have far less crime. Crime is probably more the result of four factors that at first glance seem to be the least likely causes.

The first, believe it or not, is the fact that we are a free and democratic society. Individual liberty, civil rights, and freedom from excessive controls are elements of our society that we value most and would never abandon even though they go hand-in-hand with increased crime rates. Totalitarian societies are relatively crime-free, but they pay a price in the loss of personal freedom that we would find unacceptable.

Second is what we might call The American Way. Individualism, affluence, mobility, urbanization, materialism, competition, consumerism— the defining values of our culture—each contributes in its own way to the crime picture. For example, mobility and urbanization erode community, which is our strongest bulwark against crime. Affluence, materialism, and consumerism create both desire and hopelessness among the poor, sometimes leading to criminal efforts to achieve the good life. Individualism and competition undermine social cohesion and cooperation, qualities that characterize low-crime nations such as Japan.

Third is law enforcement itself—our very efforts to control crime. Police corruption is only part of the story. More important, prisons have become training grounds for crime, detective work requires sustaining networks of criminal informants, and because we spend more money building prisons than schools, the escalating costs of incarceration have siphoned off funds that could pay for crime prevention such as education and job training.

Fourth, we suffer from the glamorization of crime and violence. As a nation we are obsessed with the excitement of crime and fascinated by violent criminals. It is not the amount of violence on television that should worry us but how violence is often shown to be the manly and ultimately the most satisfying resolution of conflict. Leading a life of crime is even seen as a road to sexual adventure, a motivational force impossible to overestimate. Inevitably, popular culture links sex and violence. As a result, gangsters, even prisoners, are shown in movies and books to have little difficulty attracting women.

Actions that would likely reduce crime are also paradoxical, opposite from what politicians propose and all of us instinctively support. Bigger prisons, more police, and harsher sentences seem rational and appealing but are often counterproductive. Rather, we should consider measures that would really help. I will mention some radical suggestions, but as professor and author Zimring points out, some of the crime reduction comes from what he calls "tinkering at the edges" like changes in management style, such as placing police out on neighborhood patrol. That should encourage designers who can surely conceive minor changes in design strategies.

In the exercise of thinking about crime, one cannot avoid some fundamental truths that place it in the category of unsolvable predicament. For example, in 1995, Los Angeles suffered more than 1,000 homicides by handguns, while in London, England, where even most of the police carry no guns, there were fewer than 100. In some countries, the statistics are even more dramatically revealing. One can only conclude that disarmament would surely be one way to make a positive difference, and complete disarmament, however unlikely, would eliminate tens of thousands of gun deaths each year. Whether partial disarmament would reduce crime is a subject of frequent and legitimate debate. But there are so many guns, more than 200 million among U.S. owners (studies show there is actually a gun in every other household), plus not only a powerful lobby that intends to keep it that way but a large segment of the populace with no intention of giving up guns just to reduce crime. We really don't care that much about reducing crime, partly for the reason I already mentioned: We are seldom touched by violent crime, and we can endure the rest.

Some kinds of technology have become so imbedded in our society—automobiles, computers, phones, and, yes, guns—that, according to philosopher of technology Langdon Winner, they have become not just ubiquitous but autonomous, no longer under our control. We could not rid ourselves of them if we tried. And plenty of people have tried. Guns own us as much as we own them.

Similarly, any thoughtful person can see that we could decriminalize or legalize much that is common behavior but is now considered criminal. Can it possibly be worth all the crime that results from our historically futile and largely hypocritical attempts to prevent people from selling sex, taking drugs, and gambling? Apparently yes. We all know that the chances of legalizing those vices, except in special locations or specific situations, are virtually nil.

And while we're thinking big, why not empty these huge, expensive, and failing prisons? Rehabilitation is impossible in the giant prisons we continue to build. Convicts emerge hardened and likely to commit more serious crimes. Even prison guards and prisoners themselves think that only a small fraction of the inmates represent any danger to society. The research clearly shows that we should keep those who must be incarcerated or who could profit from incarceration in small units of 20 people or fewer, preferably in the communities to which they will return, engaged in individually designed programs of rehabilitation. The benefits would be great and the dangers small. Will we do that? Will politicians begin to consult criminologists? Will Americans allow convicts to be housed in their communities? Will our leaders even ask them to? Doubtful.

We can make our lives safer. But all of us, especially leaders, will first have to realize that Americans do not have a crime problem. We have a crime predicament—a permanent, complicated, paradoxical dilemma. Problems have solutions, but predicaments can only be coped with. When a predicament is treated as a problem it becomes worse. Crime is no exception.

So what can design do about this ugly crime picture? If we define design as Milton Glaser does, as the introduction of intent into events, then the entire crime predicament is vulnerable to design. It may be easier to see its place in the design of prisons or communities or transportation than it is in the design of policing systems, drug programs, or disarmament, but design is called for everywhere.

The nonprofit group Architects/Designers/Planners for Social Responsibility has organized to boycott the development of all prisons because they know prisons to increase crime. They are certainly justified in making that assessment because rehabilitation in the giant prisons we now construct is virtually impossible and about half, sometimes more, of released convicts return to prison, typically having committed a more serious crime than the one that caused their previous incarceration. Moreover, it is encouraging to see a highly motivated, socially responsible action by designers, who have for years simply gone along with whatever requirements were placed upon their talents even when they were fully aware that giant prisons create crime. So if the ability to say no defines the distinction between a profession and a business, then these boycotting architects, designers, and planners have clearly established their professional posture.

It is, however, an example of the gap between design and social science that the professional action is boycotting all prison construction, when there is strong evidence that some methods of incarceration can lead to rehabilitation. But the design is radically different. Several decades ago, University of Michigan professor Theodore Newcomb, then dean of American social psychologists, showed that if groups of prisoners were kept to about 18 (instead of the hundreds or thousands now in most prisons), rehabilitation was not only possible but likely. Further studies by criminologists (who never seem to be consulted by those who continue to call for these giant prisons) show that rehabilitation programs designed for one individual at a time and reflecting the particular character and needs of that individual can achieve remarkable success. And it has long been known that if criminals can be treated in the communities to which they will return, rehabilitation is improved even further. But this knowledge has not been implemented.

Ex-convicts (or ex-offenders, as they prefer to be called) can be a major resource for crime control. Beginning in the 1960s, the Western Behavioral Sciences Institute employed a number of them. Most of them were formerly armed robbers, but there was one murderer. We organized a program led by social psychologists Wayman Crow and Rosemary Erickson to be jointly funded by the Law Enforcement Assistance Administration and 7-Eleven Inc. to see if we could reduce convenience store robberies. We found the resource these ex-offenders represented to be valuable indeed. Working as a team, they interviewed each other and some of their previous connections and came up with a number of design ideas that probably wouldn't have occurred to those of us who had never cased a site for nefarious purposes.

At the time, the windows of 7-Eleven stores were covered with large ads preventing any view of the store's interior, which of course would be ideal for the potential robber who does not want to be observed. We had them removed. On the ex-offenders' recommendation, we also moved the check stand to the front of the store, placed a telephone in plain sight, prepared a sign to place on the safe indicating that the clerk did not have access to it, and instituted a number of other such design changes. We also learned that the practice of clerks carefully observing a robber so as to be able to give a useful description to the police made the robber nervous and angry and therefore more likely to escalate the crime to violence, which, more than the loss of money, was what the study was trying to prevent. So we set up training programs to teach the staff how to be robbed.

The study became a classic in crime control literature, and the practices spread throughout the entire retail business. The application of our findings and the design recommendations we made eventually reduced the number of robberies (and the occasional violence) in tens of thousands of 7-Eleven stores by 40 percent.

The difficult issue to overcome is not the appropriateness of design intervention but getting designers to move the current boundaries of design to include these factors as legitimate areas of attention, to bridge the gap between design and the social sciences. Criminologists know a lot, but they are not building prisons, designing communities, preparing graphic messages for the media, and playing other important roles that are already played by designers, let alone the roles in social design that they could play.

Just as a mental exercise, suppose that the leadership role in the professional task of reducing crime were given to the design professions rather than to the current criminal justice system. Since the current system is working poorly (and maybe not at all), that might not be such a bad idea. That would mean our current system of police, courts, and prisons would be set aside and used only if it fit into the design of a new system. But all the money now spent on it would be available to designers—hundreds of billions of dollars.

As we already know, we could empty the prisons and not experience much additional crime. Designers then might begin to think about making possible those things that deter crime: communities where there are dozens of shops, parks, and other meeting places, the ability for citizens to know and monitor each other in neighborhoods designed to be less segregated. Incarceration, if necessary, could be accomplished in small units in the community. The public and the police would be disarmed. (I said this was just a mental exercise, remember.)

People without shelter would be provided for with new housing designs, and there would be plenty of money to help reduce the problems of the poverty stricken. The need for police in patrol cars would be reduced because we know that the crime rate goes down when police walk the beat and get involved with people in their district. When neighborhood buildings are not allowed to fall into disrepair, crime is reduced.

Voting for political leaders and legislative propositions would not be done the way it is now but through mass media designs displaying the aspects of candidates and their programs that we most need to know. And the propositions, instead of being presented as complicated and misleading descriptions on printed ballots, would be presented as alternative scenarios on television so that voters could sensibly choose among the futures that are shown, futures with less crime. Legislation and programs that then become obviously counterproductive, such as imprisoning drug addicts, would lose their support. Compare the media presentations we could make with what is now the central feature of local TV news—"If it bleeds, it leads," giving all viewers such a frightening picture of their world that heightened security keeps them from many of the very community activities that would reduce crime. The education system would be redesigned to enable people at all ages to become more knowledgeable and responsible citizens.

I could go on, but I think you see that in all the above, designers could lead. These are all design opportunities, and we have only scratched the surface.

Metadesign and Healthcare

T he United States has some of the highest technology medicine and the best trained physicians in the world. Wealthy people come from all over the world to benefit from the achievements of our medical research and development. Yet Americans are not nearly as healthy as people in almost every other advanced nation.

There are some marvelous benefits of modern medical practice, and my own life has been saved by them. However, the potential over-all effectiveness of professional medical care is countered by the fact that many practices are administered without much evidence or confidence, that people often heal by themselves, and that medicine creates about as much illness as it cures. This is largely a result of physician-induced "iatrogenic" disease due to side effects of drugs, complications from surgery, staph infections acquired in the hospital, etc. Much of the time of hospital staff is now spent treating iatrogenic disease. But perhaps an even greater problem arises from medical mistakes (such as prescribing the wrong drug, giving the wrong dosage, or amputating the wrong leg), which accounts for one-fifth of all hospital admissions (2 million cases a year), including at least 100,000 deaths. (An insurance company CEO told me that mortality is closer to 300,000.) Researchers suggest that the estimates are probably low because at least 70 percent and as many as 95 percent of adverse reactions and errors are never reported. And designers are worried about the effects of *their* mistakes!

One wonders how much of the cost of medical treatment is tied up in iatrogenic disease, medical mistakes, unnecessary surgery, and the like. One report by *Life Extension* magazine estimates the annual cost at $282 billion. *Harper's* reports that in 2005 there were 40,000 appendectomies where there was no appendicitis, and a U.S. Department of Health and Human Services report sets the number of deaths from unnecessary procedures in 2001 at 37,136.

If there is an overall positive effect of the practice of medicine, it may be so small that it could be rounded off. But it is probably worse. An accumulation of the various statistics leads one to conclude that medical practice is the leading cause of death, ahead of heart disease and cancer. We need to be reminded always that most of our better health as well as the improvements made in the number of people reaching old age result not from medical practice but from personal discipline such as diet and exercise, from public health measures including nutrition, sanitation, mosquito eradication, etc., and from the beneficial effects of human relationships and membership in a community. Some authorities hold that even the elimination of plagues was less a consequence of vaccines than it was of nutrition. Of course, it is difficult to compare national health programs since the environmental, social, and lifestyle factors are so different from culture to culture.

Noted social critic Ivan Illich wrote a book, *Medical Nemesis*, holding that the greatest threat to the health of Americans was the practice of medicine, that institutional medicine is overwhelmingly pathogenic and actively sickening. Leonard Laster, himself a distinguished physician as chancellor emeritus of the University of Massachusetts Medical School and a critic of many aspects of the medical profession, tended to qualify Illich's statement by saying that he believed the greatest threat to the health of Americans is "the way physicians lust for profits through the free market, display insensitivity to the interests of the individual patient, devalue excellence, worship at a shrine of mythical operational efficiency, and believe in the unbounded value of bigness in organizations. These attitudes have twisted and skewed the practice of medicine so that in too many ways it violates its once hallowed standards of decency and service to people."

Laster also called attention to the equally great threat to our health in the way people behave—to themselves and to others. They believe in their own immortality before they take sick. They fail to battle the slavery of addictions (tobacco, alcohol, narcotics, overeating). They fail to adopt reasonably helpful life styles (exercise and moderation). They give vent to hatred and rage and so they maim, rape, and kill. He concludes by saying, "Mr. Illich, it's really too complex for an aphorism."

The free market in medicine and in other professions and businesses is not always free, being manipulated by advertising and the actions of professional societies to limit the size of the profession through licensing, educational standards, accreditation, and other protectionist measures. This is to say nothing of the pernicious influence of pharmaceutical and health insurance companies that have shaped the practice of medicine to meet their own needs, not the needs of patients.

In addition, there is the numbers issue. If everyone in the world who has skin lesions wanted to see a doctor to have them treated, there wouldn't be enough specialists to handle even a small fraction of those affected. So we must find other solutions.

I'm reminded of the reason, back in the 1940s, Robert Hutchins, then president of the University of Chicago, wouldn't support the creation of a school of dentistry. He said that if you lined up all the dentists in the country on the East Coast and marched them westward, filling all the teeth that contained cavities, they wouldn't, in their lifetimes, get past Poughkeepsie. I actually don't remember the town, but you get the idea.

In trying to figure out what the design interventions should be to make us all healthier, one is tempted first to look at the achievements already made by design changes. For example, hundreds of thousands of lives have been saved by simply requiring hand washing to stem the spread of infections (and making that easy by installing disinfectant dispensers everywhere) and by making sure the proper procedures in surgery are meticulously followed (by requiring the surgeon and staff to follow a system checklist similar to the ones used by airplane pilots). Think what more intensive examinations of the practices could accomplish.

As I mentioned earlier, one of the more impressive findings supportive of a design approach to health is also related to hospital care. Patients simply get well sooner if they recover in a room with a view of greenery. Being in a natural setting or even viewing it through a window continues to prove amazingly beneficial to our overall health.

But we need to take a more expansive look at the design implications, and perhaps we can start with a quote from one of the Western Behavioral Sciences Institute's International Leadership Forum conferences held on these medical issues, from which Lenard Laster's comments on Ivan Illich were taken. That conference included as a participant the late Harlan Cleveland, former U.S. Ambassador to NATO and president of the University of Hawaii, who made the following entry in our discussion:

> "There's one fixing-it principle that strikes me as central to a future strategy: that the person most responsible for his or her health has to be that person (or a surrogate).

> "We do seem to be moving in that direction. Our family doctor in Minnesota repeatedly regaled me with stories about patients coming into his office with their pockets overstuffed with newspaper clippings and notes about what they had heard on television and radio. 'They're not consulting a primary physician,' he once said to me with a tolerant smile. 'They're seeking a second opinion.'

> "His judgment, and mine after thinking about it, was that the coordinator of health delivery had better be the consumer/patient. Most of what affects our health is decisions we consumers make about lifestyle, diet, exercise, stress, etc. Doctors and other specialists with special education (nurses, medical technicians, therapists, nutritionists, and many others) can help us (a) as consultants as long as we're reasonably healthy and (b) as a 'second echelon' rescue squad when we get sick enough to need them to be making the professional judgments about what to do next.

> "I confess that I haven't thought hard enough about the design of a health delivery system (and a medical education system and a public health system) that starts with consumers as coordinators of their

own health. But I have a hunch that it might persuade medical educators to put less emphasis on more and more specialization and more on integrative and interdisciplinary thinking.

"I carry in my random access memory a comment made by the dean of our medical school when (as president of the University of Hawaii) I complained in a deans meeting that in too many of our interdisciplinary courses several faculty members seemed to teach their own disciplines and it was only the students who were expected to be interdisciplinary. 'Don't take it so hard, Harlan,' said the medical dean. 'It's the same all over. In a modern urban hospital, the only generalist left is the patient.'"

Taking a patient-centered approach as a design philosophy might get us somewhere. Instead of following the top-down professional-dominated design now in place, we should entertain in all of our recommendations a bottom-up approach. Sick people and others who have been treated medically are a major resource for helping others. For example, many physically troubled people now get help from each other through extensive information and consultation available from the Internet. We can surely design other ways to help them connect with each other.

In treating mental illness, the benefits of increasing the interaction of the patients in psychiatric hospitals and, better yet, in small community-centered residences or outpatient programs would do more for most patients than professional practice. We could even include leadership roles for those capable of them. Many self-help groups succeed in illustrating that point. In addition, we need to redefine mental illness to exclude much that is often situationally determined, such as the heavily diagnosed attention deficit disorder in schoolchildren.

A former student of mine, Steven Mann, wrote a doctoral dissertation on the meaning of illness to the patient. In his research interviewing many patients, Mann discovered that a number of patients reported that through some deep inner process they were actually shaping their own illnesses, deliberately making themselves better or worse—moving themselves sometimes toward more serious illness, even to the brink of disaster, and sometimes away from it. This psychological process was seemingly independent from the medicine or treatment they were receiving. Interestingly, they never mentioned this phenomenon to their physicians. Clearly, there is much to study, not just about the mind and the diseased body but also about the complicated physician-patient relationship.

Moreover, we need to know more about the introduction of lay-men into the constellation of helpful relationships such as the intensive use of trained volunteers in hospice treatment.

There are certainly technological solutions to extending practice. Physicians have long used telephone conversations to reach patients to give them progress reports or to aid them in times of desperate need.

To what extent can the Internet be called into play? Millions of sick people now first consult the Web for information from databases and advice from those who suffer the same symptoms. In many cases, that procedure has led to the patient knowing more about a specific disease than does the doctor. I don't know to what extent that process might be better organized and led by physicians. Three ancient but valid concerns present themselves—the physician's need to see the patient up close, the therapeutic effect of the laying on of hands, and the curative power of the physicians' mystique and physical presence. Maybe all of those can be handled by technology (even the laying on of hands!) but no doubt there will be resistance. I find it in myself. I'm not for automating or robotizing everything, but I am for designing almost everything.

Perhaps we can play another imagination game, a mental exercise putting designers in leadership. Suppose there were no physicians or hospitals or drug companies. How might designers protect us from ill-ness and improve our health?

To begin with, the emphasis would be on building relationships, which is the best protection against illness. As we've seen, many physical and social designs would promote that kind of work. Again, the devel-opment of community plays a major role. Designs can also promote exercise by creating sidewalks and trails, making bicycles safer and easier to ride and gyms available in homes and neighborhoods. Exposure to greenery and to nature in general would be extremely beneficial.

Volunteer self-help groups that encourage the personal discipline required for dietary control and other health measures would be useful, too. These could be developed hand-in-hand with mass media educational programs about healthful practices, giving TV audiences a different picture from the one they now see in which prescription drug advertisements dominate commercial television. The prevention of accidents, which are a major factor in crippling illness and death, particularly for children and the elderly, could be a most worthwhile challenge for designers.

Perhaps the most beneficial designs would be those that reduce stress, which is probably a factor in the majority of illnesses. Stress is developed in poorly designed work environments and crowded highways and also among increasingly overburdened parents who because they fear letting their children use inadequate public transportation devote much of their time to serving and monitoring their children.

When you think about it, there is a whole world of design opportunity that could create a healthier population.

Metadesign and Education

One frequent criticism of American education is that it has not fundamentally changed in several centuries. Regrettably, the criticism that holds that if you're doing what you were trained to do, you're obsolete, does not seem to apply to teaching.

Education has withstood almost every effort to bring about radical change. Even technology, which has changed almost every other profession, has yet to change elementary and secondary schooling. The inventions that many thought would transform education have essentially come and gone—or more accurately, been subsumed into the traditional form of education. The "magic lantern" slide projector, radio, film, television, video, computers—none has had the impact it was expected to have.

Like the history of fighting wars with China, where the invading victors were simply absorbed by that giant culture, a parade of educational reformers have sought to bring about fundamental change only to discover that their successes faded while the existing system remained intact.

Education reformers often find that they can indeed transform a classroom, even a school, but upon returning a year later discover that the great experiment has disappeared, and the status quo has returned. I have spent time with several of them who were able to greatly increase the interaction of students, creating enhanced peer learning, but within months the experiment faded. One of them told me, "It's like kicking a huge mountain of mashed potatoes. It's easy to make a dent, but somehow the dent just slowly disappears."

That resistance to change might be considered a strength if we could believe that the traditional format has survived these powerful technological interventions because it is such a fundamentally sound system, so reliably effective, so demonstrably rewarding to students, teachers, and society. But as demonstrated through high dropout rates, massive functional illiteracy among high school graduates, and the need for remedial education of college freshmen, America's students are falling far behind those of other countries in practically every field. Add to this that half of all teachers leave the field after less than five years in what many thought would be a career profession. It's hard to say that American education is working all that well.

As disturbing and possibly discouraging as this picture is, there is an even more challenging factor to deal with. Ever since the 1966 Equality of Educational Opportunity Study (also known as the Coleman study) revealed why there was such a gap between blacks and whites in academic achievement, we have had to come to terms with the fact that socioeconomic class is more determining of what students learn than is anything offered in schools. What happens in communities and families accounts for about two-thirds of the problems, with schooling accounting for the rest.

Since racial segregation in schools and communities is still with us almost in the same form as it was at the time of that study, we really have our work cut out for us. But in a sense, it plays into the hands of designers because as Richard Rothstein writes in his book *Class and Schools*, the steps that need to be taken and that Americans seem unwilling to take are precisely those with which designers often work: housing, transportation, zoning, and other urban policies. We need to see these as education issues. Changes in those design policies could permit what Rothstein insists is necessary to close that gap: permitting families of different classes to live in close proximity so their children can attend the same neighborhood schools. A more even mixture of black and white students greatly affects the abilities of blacks to achieve.

So the answer is not only in school reforms but in broader programs of social change. For Rothstein, low wages for working parents with children, poor healthcare (low-income families have less access to medical care here than in any other industrialized nation), inadequate housing, and lack of opportunity for high-quality early childhood, after-school, and summer activities are all educational problems. I would add that to a significant extent they are design problems.

While socioeconomic class is powerfully determining, schools do remain important, and if we are going to motivate all students to much higher performance we will have to undertake projects that make use of the most powerful influences we know about. First among these is the fact that students learn from each other—a fact that is too often ignored in the design of education. A former U.S. Commissioner of Education told a small group of us privately that he felt the most important fact emerging from education research is that students at every level, from kindergarten through graduate school, learn more from each other than from their teachers. If the situation is conducive, they also learn from themselves. These resources should be the main considerations in designing new programs.

We must also look at the negative effects of constant judgment. Rothstein points out that we cannot expect higher standards, more testing, improved accountability, and better school leadership to improve student achievement. Rather, we must improve the learning situations, which is what designers do. One resource we can employ is the use of volunteer laypeople as aides and tutors. That means we must get teachers unions to relax their protectionist concern and realize that all teachers will have to become metaprofessionals, teachers of teachers. We will never have enough teachers to do the job if we insist that every student needs to be dealt with by a professionally trained teacher. Teaching, like every profession, must become a metaprofession, one of managing lay resources.

In that way, we can essentially reduce class size, which has proven to be important, and raise teachers' pay at the same time. But we will have to relax our insistence that all students learn exactly the same things. We want them to learn voraciously, just as they did before they went to school.

Still, teachers play a crucial role. But it isn't the role that most people, including teachers, think they play. It's a much richer, more profound role because their scripted performance is not what their students learn. Teaching is like parenthood. What parents deliberately *do* in terms of parenting skills matters little in what their children become. But what parents *are* matters a great deal. That is what children learn and become. Children always learn who their parents really are, even if the parents sometimes wish that weren't so. The same is true for teachers. Students learn who their teachers are, and that can be highly influential in many directions.

That's why it is unfortunate that teachers are saddled with so many curricular goals and disciplinary burdens instead of being able to express themselves and their own strong interests. It is especially discouraging to note that teachers are increasingly frustrated by having to place discipline ahead of teaching and engage in practices they know are unsupported by research, such as grading, homework, and curricular limitations that are politically mandated. Teachers probably would not choose to be constantly in an evaluative relationship to their students.

Yet evaluation seems so rational. After all, how can students know how they are doing without evaluation? And how would we make decisions about extending contracts or giving tenure without evaluation? How else can we hold people in the system accountable? The rational defense of evaluation seems overwhelming. But human affairs do not operate rationally. They operate paradoxically. In human experience, paradox is the rule, not the exception. Rational evaluation is always likely to be off the mark.

Every teacher knows that Albert Einstein and Thomas Edison did not do well in school and that Bill Gates and Steve Jobs dropped out of college, but they can seldom apply that understanding to their current students. Indeed, the system hardly lets them.

What all of us need—students, teachers, and administrators—is not evaluation but engagement. We need to be encouraged to take risks, and when the effort doesn't work or a mistake is made, we don't need judgment, we need understanding. We need to analyze the failure in the company of our teacher (or the teacher in the company of the administrator) and see what can be learned from it. That is what better teachers and better bosses have always done. Evaluation is cheap and easy and superficial. Engagement is more demanding but far more rewarding.

The emphasis on accountability and evaluation in schooling produces a situation in which students simply do not learn much of what is in the curriculum. Studies show that because their learning is mostly cramming for tests, students retain little of what they learn, failing tests they passed just two weeks earlier. I attended an education conference where a speaker reported on a study in which students passed a test in the morning, went to lunch, and failed it in the afternoon.

Naturally, we want teachers who know the subject being taught, but perhaps even more, we need teachers who know something of interest to share with students, whether it is in the standard curriculum or not—astronomy, bird watching, dancing, environmental management, whatever. We need teachers who can make learning exciting because they themselves are excited. In that process we learn that there are many avenues to the basics.

Having said that, I do want to recognize the place and structure of subject matter that has been deemed important for centuries as well as the dedicated work of some extraordinary educators who have organized curricular material in ways that make it accessible. But to have those resources, we do not need evaluation as it is now practiced. If we deem it important that students receive feedback on their progress (which they seldom need because they already know how they're doing), it is possible to make that feedback self-administered or automated, removing the teacher and the student from the dysfunctional evaluative relationship and the oppressive grading system.

The great lesson in leadership and design is to recognize the natural coexistence of opposites, of freedom and limits, and the inevitable paradoxes in life. The best leaders are able to go in seemingly opposite directions at once. Yes, we need teachers who bring something special of themselves to the learning situation. In addition, we need organization, the discipline of a curriculum, and attention to subject matter that has stood the test of time. These concerns are not mutually exclusive. There is even a term for it: simultaneous management.

Architects and other designers, in constructing so many thousands of schools (several new ones are opened every day in the United States) have made important contributions, even though it would seem that the major features of classroom design have remained pretty much consistent for generations, providing arrangements that serve about 30 students per classroom, organized by grade, with a teacher presiding.

But there are changes. Increasingly, students are clustered in groups that tend to work in some collaboration. There was a time when, for security reasons or to eliminate distraction, windows were eliminated. Since then we have discovered that in rooms with windows, people are smarter.

It is also important to keep in mind that much of what is done by students and teachers in schools, often demanded by school boards or parents, has been shown to be irrelevant or counterproductive. Homework, grades, rewards, and punishments, for example, are not related to improved learning. Evaluation procedures, and there are a lot of them, are useful only for management, for example, deciding who gets promoted to the next grade (even though clustering by grades is not necessarily a proven design).

To conclude this chapter, I would like to present the following list of considerations to be attended to by those wanting to redesign education. It was generated in a conference of the Fellows in the Western Behavioral Sciences Institute's International Leadership Forum:

- The program should be broadly community based, involving a wide variety of organizations and institutions, not limited to schools.
- An emphasis should be placed on the arts, humanities, and social sciences because they are more likely to lead to better citizenship, greater maturity, and the achievement of wisdom.
- The educational system should not be limited to children but be designed as a lifelong experience.

- Many educational options in addition to schools, such as apprenticeships, exchange programs, interning, adventures, entrepreneurial programs, mentoring, travel, and public service, should be available and funded on an equal footing with schools.
- Schools can be organized to offer different curricular emphases, such as magnet schools do now.
- Education should be non-compulsory, and all programs should respect children's rights and self-determination—ranging from freedom from corporal punishment to the right to justice and political and economic power. Discriminatory programs based on age differences, however applied to young and old, should be eliminated. As an alternative, a student or a student/parent combination could petition to be relieved of compulsory school attendance if that petition, based on a creative design for an alternative path, were approved for funding at the level of current per student allocations. The design would have to meet certain criteria but could be broadly conceived.
- To the extent possible, all students should be able to determine their own educational goals and design their own educational experiences. The programs should be organized to respect and accommodate individual differences.
- There must be a time limit to daily, weekly, and annual learning demands (and opportunities).
- All citizens age four and over should be given a basic lifelong "national learning tuition grant" that they can use or lose on an annual basis. When they use it, they are given paid leave from work. Unemployed people are paid a stipend for completing these learning opportunities.
- The overall design should recognize that we are undergoing what Margaret Mead called a reverse transmission of culture in which young people have much to teach the older generations. That is particularly evident in the digital revolution.
- The design should make strong use of peer learning, recognizing the fact that students at all levels, from kindergarten through

graduate school, have always learned more from each other than from teachers.

- The overall plan should build on the fact that the Internet makes possible an entirely new social form, one enabling nongeographic global communities.
- Not all education should be targeted to the individual. Since people increasingly live and work and learn in various ensembles, some aspects of the educational experience would sensibly be directed to constellations of people—families, student networks, work groups, etc.
- We need to build virtual learning communities as a basic element in providing learning opportunities.
- De-emphasize evaluation and recognize the need for tinkering, risk-taking, and innovation, which guarantee a considerable number of failure experiences.
- Special attention must be paid to making room for genius to emerge, as our civilization is at least as dependent on creative break-throughs as it is on general literacy.
- With regard to accountability, the design must recognize that the greatest ideas, the ones most likely to make a fundamental contribution to civilization's progress, will at first and perhaps for decades be ignored, ridiculed, or hated.
- The design should provide for open learning communities, which would be essentially leaderless.
- The plan should recognize that not all learning will be along conventional lines, of studying only words on a page, but may well include activities more like graphic learning, editing videos and films, and navigation skills on the Web.
- Attention must be paid to people's physical readiness for learning, which is influenced by rest, exercise, and good nutrition.
- Although it is still practiced in 23 states, corporal punishment should be forbidden as a disciplinary measure in schools and in any other institution or agency included in this design.

Educational reformers tend to work individually or in small groups, which may account for their impotence in making the changes that so many people recognize as important. Teachers unions are devoted, as are all professional societies, to protectionism and are usually too fearful of what changes might do to teachers' pay and security to experiment with radical redesigns. But the informed and passionate effort of a major cluster of relevant professions such as the field of design represents just might have a chance.

Part III
Design for Human Liberation

We have started to look at the big picture, at the major social institutions we thought we knew and could count on but don't work as we need them to. They obviously require our serious design attention. In Part Three, we look at an even bigger picture as we examine how designers can create completely new social arrangements to correct conditions that limit and oppress us, that keep us from living up to our full potential as human beings. As we will see, liberation is not only an issue for certain groups but is required for everyone. In one way or another, our social and physical environments prevent it for all of us. Design has already been a major liberating force in certain areas and can be everywhere.

How Design Can
Imprison or Free Us

Designers don't often think of their work in political terms. I'm not referring to partisan politics but to the politics of personal and social liberation. Yet practically every design decision is in a sense a political decision. Every act reinforces or redistributes power. It either increases or reduces the freedom and leverage of individuals and groups. Designs, whether conscious or inadvertent, liberate or constrain those who are influenced by them.

Take, for example, the design achievements over the past few decades in serving that huge segment of America's population that had been ignored for centuries: the disabled. Through leadership and legislation, building upon the new consciousness of the civil rights movement and cooperating with advocates of the disabled and politicians sensitive to the cause, designers have greatly increased the access and mobility of this population, thereby liberating them for fuller participation in society.

Thanks to the work of many kinds of designers, millions of previously ignored citizens have been empowered so that they can enjoy life in a way denied them throughout history. Some designs were relatively simple to engineer, such as designated parking places for people unable to walk or move long distances and roomy restroom stalls with toilets and all the accommodating features placed within reach. Other designs are technologically complex and sophisticated, such as electronic prostheses that serve as limbs where they would otherwise be missing and vehicles specially designed to transport wheelchair occupants. Designs that may seem simply handy to the general population, such as an implement to help unscrew the tight lid of a jar, can, for someone with arthritis, make the difference between being able to live independently and having to rely on constant assistance.

Occasionally, a design to liberate one population inadvertently helps liberate another. When public telephones and drinking fountains were lowered to serve people in wheelchairs, children were also accommodated. The same kind of service to children came with the improved entry into buses and other public vehicles redesigned for the disabled.

Now that we are getting used to ramps and toilets that accommodate people who use wheelchairs, it all seems so sensible. It's hard to imagine how we could have ignored this population for so long. But we forget that while we knew wheelchair users existed, they were essentially invisible to many of us, marginalized partly by the way they were ignored in previous design considerations. That is the case with all liberation movements. We think we know these people until we have our consciousness raised, and then we see more clearly how designs have limited them. That has been true of all civil rights movements. The design implications are most clearly evident with the disabled, but they are true also for the liberation of women, ethnic groups, and soon perhaps for that one-third of our population that is discriminated against in every area of life—children and youth.

We are embarrassed to have spent a century designating separate drinking fountains for people of color, but there were and perhaps still are designs that similarly insult, oppress, and limit the potential of other groups as well. Offices designed for the almost entirely female contingent of secretaries and clerical assistants—essentially windowless interior spaces that used to be referred to pejoratively as "hen houses"—while male executives enjoyed the privacy of offices with windows, surely served to limit the access of women to management roles. Rules—or we might call them designs—created by men, were presumably meant to protect women, such as requiring management to provide coffee breaks and forbidding women to be worked overtime or to hold jobs that required heavy lifting and requiring cots in ladies' restrooms but not in men's. These served not to protect women but to prevent them from advancing to leadership roles. The rationale (the metamessage) was that women were too fragile to undertake the more demanding work of management. Women, who still earn significantly less than men, were essentially "protected" into poverty.

That is why we have civil rights—to protect us from good people who think they know what's best for us—blacks from whites, women from men, employees from bosses, children from parents, people from government. Tyrants have always acted in the best interests of their people, or so they thought.

But designers are making a difference. Now when we men visit an airport restroom, we are likely to see space set up to accommodate a diaper change. The communication that child care is not exclusively a woman's responsibility is a powerful liberating message, backed up by a facilitating design. When I mentioned to an architect friend that we have research showing that when families eat dinner together five nights a week, the children are far less likely to fail in school, get in trouble with the law, and suffer other consequences of family dysfunction, he thought that there might be ways to encourage that dinner arrangement by design.

He pointed out that we might begin to see house designs that are not as territorially determined as they are now, with women placed in the kitchen, fathers and children in the family room, and nobody in the dining room. Perhaps kitchens could be arranged to promote the combined effort of the family in preparing the meal and then sitting down together to enjoy it. That would partially liberate the mother (who has probably worked at another job all day) from the cook's role and serve to improve family life in other ways as well.

I find it illuminating to construct what we might call a liberation design matrix. Along the horizontal axis at the top we list all the identifiable groups that make up our society and for whom we might design better lives if we understood their particular circumstances: African-American, Hispanic, Asian, Native American, women, men, children, elderly, gay, disabled, homeless, those held in prisons, psychiatric hospitals, nursing homes, schools, and so on. On the vertical axis down the left side we could list various design categories: media, housing, advertising, offices, criminal justice, transportation, education, parenthood, healthcare, urban design, etc. The third dimension in our two-dimensional matrix would have to be imagined—a representation of each of the design professions: architecture, graphic design, interior design, industrial design, cyberspace design, landscape architecture, urban planning, etc.

My guess is that with enough time we could call up examples to fit every one of the cells in the matrix, but for illustrative simplicity, let me mention just a few.

At the juncture of women/advertising/graphic design we have already learned not to show a woman opening an oven door, preferring to show her in a professional pursuit so as not to imprison her in a stereotyped role. At men/criminal justice/architecture we have the need to design protection for new prisoners from rape in prison. At children/parenthood/interior design we are reminded that much of the high-end furniture so desired by designers and their clients with its costly finishes, upholstery, and more seriously, its dangerously sharp edges, has made parenthood extremely frustrating or worrisome as parents must put foam rubber around their designer coffee tables to protect newly walking infants. At homeless/housing/urban design we find the need to provide affordable shelter for countless thousands of homeless people in cities, in particular the hypercities growing so rapidly around the world, where 500 people share one toilet. And so on. I will treat in more detail a single special area, the liberation of children and youth, in the next chapter.

The point is that there is a universal need for design attention in every imaginable area of society, most of which are matters of serious public concern and would appropriately be supported by taxpayers, as they have supported designs for the disabled. What may be hard for designers to accept is that no professions can do as much to promote the liberation of oppressed groups (and there is no group in the center of society—even healthy white males over six feet tall—that is not in some way oppressed) as can the professions of design.

12

Designs for the Liberation of Children and Youth

I n the 1960s during the heat of the civil rights movement, I figured out something quite helpful in thinking about what was happening. I'm sure others had figured it out too, but they hadn't told me. It's this: If you want to predict which group in our society will mount a movement for their liberation, don't look to those people for whom you feel most sorry. Instead, look to the ones for whom you don't feel at all sorry.

The reasons liberation movements always take us by surprise is that we think the people rebelling were doing just fine. As white Americans used to say about blacks, "They are happy in their place." Similarly, men were stunned when women protested because men thought women had it made, were well protected, adored, placed on a pedestal, had doors opened for them, and their cigarettes lit. What on earth could they want?

In 1966, before the modern women's movement got started but the civil rights movement was well underway, I was a speaker at a conference of more than 2,000 women in New York titled Quo Vadis Today's Woman (Where is today's woman going?). Sitting on the stage with me were the three other speakers: John Mack Carter, then editor of *Ladies' Home Journal*, Ashley Montagu, the noted anthropologist, and Eli Ginsberg, a professor of economics at New York University. I recall looking down that lineup of male speakers and thinking, "My God. I cannot imagine this situation in reverse: 2,000 men gathered at a conference under the title Quo Vadis Today's Man, listening to four women tell them where they are going. That was the moment that a new consciousness clicked for me, and I realized our discriminatory attitudes toward women were more deeply entrenched than they were even with ethnic groups and that there surely would be a women's liberation movement.

I began then to take a serious look beyond the stereotypes and studied the way women actually lived. I discovered what they were beginning to discover: They were victims of extensive oppression, justifying just the kind of protest movement that was eventually generated. In 1969 I wrote an article about it, the first to appear in a national magazine (*Look*).

If women were justified in mounting a liberation movement, I wondered, what about children? They outnumber women, and when I studied their situation, I discovered that they were even more limited, oppressed, and mistreated—clearly prevented from living up to their full potential. The image all of us had of childhood as a time of innocent, carefree, happy lives was not the case.

What can designers do about that? Plenty. But to understand it better, let's begin with another paradox. Children are our No. 1 subject of conversation. Americans talk more about children than about sports or money or movies or any other subject. We in the United States could hardly be more concerned about children than we are. Anthropologist Mary Ellen Goodman, author of *The Culture of Childhood*, puts it this way: "We have set a new record; no other people seems ever to have been so preoccupied with children, so anxious about them, or so uncertain of how to deal with them." But while parents obviously love their offspring, as a society we actually treat children, particularly teenagers, with less consideration and often with more hostility than do other nations.

Our world is not a good place for children. Discrimination against them seems to have no bounds. They are excluded from almost everything. They are segregated, ignored, impotent. Every institution in our society seems to be organized against them. We all feel that it is either natural   or   necessary   to   cooperate   in   that   discrimination.

Unconsciously, we carry out the will of a society that holds a limited and demeaned view of children and youth, one that refuses to recognize their right to full citizenship and full humanity.

To the extent that we spend time with children, we spend it protecting, teaching, controlling, and disciplining them in the service of institutions that too often care little about their interests. We must continually protect our children from speeding automobiles. We serve oppressive compulsory schools by guaranteeing that children make progress toward becoming standardized educational products. We control them so that in stores or restaurants (almost all of which are designed only for adults) children don't act like children. We discipline children so that they will blindly obey adult authority whenever it is encountered. Youths entirely capable of responsible voting or driving or being out after 10 p.m. are denied those fundamental freedoms.

In the 1970s, when our consciousness was raised about the need for expanded civil rights for women, the disabled, and ethnic groups, there was also a nascent movement for the liberation of children. I was a part of that movement and wrote a book, *Birthrights: A Bill of Rights for Children*, calling for the full protection of the U.S. Constitution for this oppressed group.

Ironically, however, a different kind of protection of children came to pass, which not only failed to liberate them but actually became more oppressive. As women painfully discovered in their own movement for liberation, protection can be the enemy of freedom. It's the same with children. Americans have become excessively fearful about children and obsessed with their protection ... from everything. Fears of injury have led to playgrounds being closed or redesigned to remove challenging equipment such as jungle gyms, manual merry-go-rounds, swings, high slides, seesaws, and the like. Irrational and unfounded fears of child predators have led to adults being unable even to speak to children they don't know, let alone tie their shoes or button their jackets. An illustrated booklet put out by the Catholic Church warns children never to be alone in a room with an adult. Always let someone know where you are and make sure the door is open, the booklet advises. All this has led to the reinvention of parenthood, which has become almost impossibly burdensome. There is a better way, and design can be redirected to liberate rather than limit children and youth.

In that quest we have to prepare ourselves to think quite differently about children than we have previously. Take voting, for example. The German parliament has considered a plan to lower the voting age to birth. That may seem absurd and shocking (although I did propose it in *Birthrights*), but it may actually serve society very well. The Germans are concerned that the growing body of elderly and their consequent increase in voting power is making family life more difficult. The elderly, for example, don't tend to vote for education improvements. To strengthen the family, the German government is looking at proposals that would lower the voting age to birth, with parents acting as proxies for their children under 12 unless the children have petitioned to vote on their own. This would increase the political power of children and of families, enabling much legislation that would benefit society in important ways.

While it is always crucial that understanding precede design, with respect to design for liberation a different level of understanding is required. Beyond knowing just the facts, we have to overcome stereotypes that are deeply embedded in us. It becomes necessary for each of us to raise our consciousness about the oppressed group because I can guarantee that just as lowering the voting age to zero seems at first crazy, we will encounter seeming absurdities operative in every area that challenge our lifelong beliefs and attitudes.

Opportunities exist in every area of our society for respecting children's and young people's rights through design by addressing juvenile justice, education, healthcare, information, economic power, sexual freedom, corporal punishment, political power, and home life, but to cover them properly requires a book, not a chapter, as I discovered.

If visitors from another planet were to happen upon an uninhabited American city, they would never guess that children existed. They would think our world was populated entirely by people five and a half to six feet tall because the entire constructed world is designed to that scale.

Only in places used exclusively by children, such as classrooms and playgrounds, do we find facilities built to their scale, evidence that children are simply not in mind during the design process, or worse, not wanted. I'm afraid it is too often the latter.

Consider a small child's day. It begins with a shower under an uncontrollable waterfall pouring down from several feet overhead; gripping the edges of the toilet seat, afraid of falling in and being washed away; unable to reach the cabinet or the sink; trying to see in a mirror placed so high that it is an impossible task. No wonder the child doesn't look the way we want. And that's before even leaving the bathroom. Soon the child must go out into the world to try to open doors that are too heavy, negotiate stairs that are too steep, reach items on shelves that are too high, pass through turnstiles that hit directly in the face, negotiate confusing cafeteria lines, ride on dangerous school buses, see a film almost totally obscured by the back of the auditorium seat in front, bang into sharp corners, risk injury in a revolving door. Is it any wonder that the child comes to feel that everything is made for adults, that adults are more important?

Writing in 1892, Kate Wiggin described the predicament of the small child in her book *Children's Rights and Others*:

"The child has a right to a place of his own, to things of his own, to surroundings which have some relation to his size, his desires, and his capabilities.

"How should we like to live, half the time, in a place where the piano was twelve feet tall, the doorknobs at an impossible height, and the mantle a shelf in the sky; where every mortal thing was out of reach except a collection of highly interesting objects on dressing tables and bureaus, guarded, however, by giants and giantesses, three times as large and powerful as ourselves, ever saying 'mustn't touch;' and if we did touch we should be spanked and have no other method of revenge save to spank back symbolically on the inoffensive person of our dolls.

"Things in general are so disproportionate to the child's stature, so far from his organs of prehension, so much above his horizontal line of vision, so much ampler than his immediate surroundings, that there is, between him and all these things, a gap to be filled only by a microcosm of playthings which give him his first object lessons."

Seeing a drinking fountain placed at a convenient height for children, a more common occurrence these days, does remind us of the presence of children, even if it may have been lowered to serve wheelchair users. Having more such physical reminders that there are children in the world would help make us more alert and attentive toward them, making their lives safer and more interesting. The real advance for children will come when adults recognize them as an integral part of the community, expecting them to be around, naturally looking out for them, and when they are freed to explore the world because of its responsive design.

Forcing children to cope with an oversized world may have created hidden as well as obvious limitations for them. There is an interesting parallel in the way we treat left-handedness. Countries that provide for left-handedness tend to have much more of it than countries that do not. In countries of the former Soviet Union, only 4 percent of the population is left-handed, while in the United States where we are more accepting of it, the figure is 16 percent. Compare these relatively low figures with those of Denmark, where over 40 percent of the population is left-handed. In a country such as Denmark, being left-handed is not considered a negative trait. The word "sinister," meaning both "evil" and "left," does not exist in their language, the furniture catalogues regularly list models in right- and left-handed styles, and there are as many left-handed scissors as right-handed ones. We can only assume that the responsive environment has allowed something to develop that might not otherwise have appeared. It makes one wonder what we might be missing, having engineered our world to fit only adults.

The politics of childhood is clearly evident when one visits a child care center—even a newly constructed "model center" that is supposedly designed for optimal use by children. One does indeed see small tables and chairs and cabinets accessible to children, but in almost no other way is the facility designed for them. From looking at the arrangement, it is apparent what the people who run the institution want the children to do—stay at their work tables and put their things away. Only the facilities necessary for these activities are designed to their scale. As in most classrooms, the teacher is provided with blackboards and bulletin boards, displaying the children's work at heights reaching all the way to the ceiling but not to the floor. The areas where important decisions are made are for adults only. Children are not even admitted to, let alone accommodated in, the kitchen or the administrative headquarters. The facility is designed for ease of adult supervision and control. Children are there to do the assigned curriculum and to follow the adult schedule. All decisions are made by adults, even those that affect children directly. The politics of childhood remains the same from one institution to the next.

Facilities do exist, however, that accommodate children as well as the adults who work with them. I once visited such a place, the child care program at a California-based rehabilitation center for drug addicts and their families. In their facility one experienced a world designed to make life better for children. Blackboards and mirrors go all the way to the floor and the shelving is low, displaying all kinds of materials with which children can engage in fantasy play. Upon entering, an adult feels the difference immediately. It is not a feeling of being a giant in a world built for much smaller people because it is certainly not uncomfortable for an adult, but it gives a sense that one has never been in such a place. One realizes instantly that it is a place for children as well as adults.

The accommodation to children was particularly evident in the nursery, where children from 6 to 18 months spend their time. In most facilities, one would see cribs set at an adult height to make it easy to handle and control the children while at the same time imprisoning them and making them dependent on adults for freedom. Instead, sleeping pallets on the carpeted floor make it possible for children of any age to climb in and out of bed and have free access to other children and other parts of the room. The teacher is not accommodated in the traditional way but can often be found seated on the floor with the children telling stories, playing, or singing. Simple design decisions have created new freedom and mobility for the children, if not for the adults. Consistent with the rest of the design for children, the meeting rooms where plans and decisions are made are as accessible to children as adults, and they participate as freely.

Unfortunately, examples of bad design for children far outnumber examples of good design. The basic problem is that even the "good" examples are not always good politically because they are found only where adults think children should be. This reflects our idea that childhood should be a time of isolation from adults. M. Paul Friedberg, the noted landscape architect who has designed some of America's most remarkable and widely acclaimed playgrounds, admits that much as he enjoys creating playgrounds, he believes that segregating children into them is not ultimately the best design solution. He holds that more of the world now denied to children should be made available to them. But design that gives children equal access to facilities ordinarily thought to be only for adults is still largely nonexistent.

The occasional appearance of good design for children serves only to remind us how often such facilities are missing. Special zoos have been designed for children, permitting them to see clearly and to touch the animals. Doors and gates are scaled to their size, making them easy to open. This is in contrast to most zoos, where the child's view is seriously impaired by fences, railings, and hedges, making it virtually impossible to see without the aid of an adult. Even in the best of children's zoos, the telephones, food and drink counters, and vending machines are placed for the convenience of adults, which means that the important functions of communication and the expenditure of money are, as usual, left to adults.

One can look almost anywhere and discover that facilities for children are either absent or inadequate. Even in places where one might reasonably expect to find children, such as in stores, restaurants, and libraries, there is little responsive design. In business, industry, hospitals, stores, symphony halls, and other places, children are almost totally excluded. Some restaurants do provide booster seats, high chairs, special bibs, and napkins for small children, but with the exception of a few family restaurants, most cater to adults only and children are somehow out of place. Markets have shopping baskets with seats for children, but this babysitting device does more than carry the child, it prevents him from "getting into things," and keeps him a virtual prisoner.

It would be possible to redesign supermarket shelves in the form of bins mounted on a Ferris wheel-like arrangement that the small child (or the person in a wheelchair) could pull down to obtain the item desired. Instead, supermarkets now place some items such as children's cereal boxes where children can see them and possibly knock them down, increasing the pressure on parents to buy them. Children as consumers are exploited rather than served.

The child's problem comes into focus when we examine the $22 billion U.S. toy industry. For all the pleasure toys can bring, they also play a part in the discrimination against children. Toys for children did not even exist until children became segregated and adults began to develop an antipathy toward them. While there are a few examples of toys dating from ancient Egypt, it is likely that until the 17th century, most toys were used also by adults. One of the first toys to be made exclusively for children was the hobby horse.

Both the structure and content of most toys reflect a demeaned view of children. Many toys are both dangerous and cheaply made. Product safety agencies are always after their makers. And because children are denied access to the real world, toys create a miniature world in which they can participate without threatening adults. They can play war games and graphically and technologically sophisticated video games, learn to cook and clean, and even engage in business—but only at the level of play.

Too often toys are used as babysitters. Giving a child a toy is like telling him to watch television. Toys can also convey a materialistic view of life, selling the child on the American ideal that accumulating things is the path to happiness. And the toy store's arsenal of weaponry, its glamorization of war and violence and its development of a cops-and-robber mentality in children is all too well known.

Although there are some new legal restraints on the manufacture and advertising of toys, it cannot be said that any major improvements are likely to come in the way of toys made or sold. But making the world safe and accessible to children is a challenge worthy of the talents of toy manufacturers. If they put themselves on the side of children politically, the books, films, and television programs they control could help raise the consciousness and the power of children. Now their efforts are almost entirely in the opposite direction.

Billions of dollars are now spent on television advertising for children, all too often making toys seem something other than what they are. The child's disappointment when the toy does not live up to expectations is such an old story with parents that some even argue this may be the best education of all: to learn not to trust what people tell you on television.

Children need the right to information, particularly the kind that might make adults nervous. Yet libraries still set aside books and articles they deem inappropriate for children and deny their access to them. At some time, practically every major literary figure has been censored: Shakespeare, Hemmingway, Twain. The history of libraries serving children and youth is not one to be proud of. But there are new efforts to make libraries work more effectively for teenagers.

An example is designer and youth rights activist Anthony Bernier's TeenS'cape development at the Los Angeles County Library, which has led to a 26 percent jump in computer use and an even greater rise in reading material circulation. The 3,780-square-foot area has been designed to welcome the teenage visitor through differences in lighting, carpeting, a sound system playing pulsed jazz, wall alcoves for privacy, cushy lounge furniture, floor seating, round tables, and three canvas-roofed small group study areas. It reflects a completely different perspective on what a library for youth should offer.

University of California Berkeley architect Galen Cranz reports favorably on a related effort at Oakland's Cesar E. Chavez Library, a lively design making it possible for the youths to vary their postures frequently, a healthful as well as inviting aspect. Some of the design allows "perching," a sit-stand posture that is considered physiologically beneficial because it allows the legs to rest while retaining the spine's curves. Included are large, deep, upholstered benches than can accommodate six people, lying down or across each other's laps or piling up like puppies on a large carpeted, elevated disc. Quite a design departure.

Toys, television, libraries, and the lack of facilities in children's scale offer only the most obvious examples from very different media of both failures and possibilities in what we generally regard as the field of design. But there are more dramatic and painful issues in the area of social design. Take, as examples, the right to physical mobility and alternative home environments.

A system that not only excludes children but is positively designed against them is transportation, the whole problem of a child's mobility. Children cannot move about in safety. They must always be under the watchful eyes of parents or of some other responsible adult because to leave them on their own is to invite injury or death. The child cannot easily make forays into the community, and the parents live in continual anxiety about the child's well-being.

The villain, of course, is the automobile and the many accommodations we have made to it. The automobile is the No. 1 enemy of children. It has transformed our villages into sprawling, polluted cities and made pedestrian travel useless, difficult, and dangerous. Each year it kills 40,000 people in the United States and injures more than 2 million others, including a high percentage of children. More than any other single factor, the automobile has changed the way we live and the way we relate to each other.

The automobile first made possible and now makes necessary the separation of work centers from commercial, residential, and recreational centers, requiring a mobility that children and many others in our society simply do not have.

Because automobiles can be legally operated only by adults, children are made more dependent. Cars are so lethal that only children over the age of 7 or 8 are typically permitted to go anywhere on foot or bicycle; even then there is still much for parents to worry about. While automobiles increase the mobility of adults, they reduce the mobility of children. Automobiles actually prevent children from exploring their world and from safely joining in the activities of the community.

Authorities in London, England, were concerned that the number of children killed as pedestrians had doubled in recent years. After intensive study they concluded, believe it or not, that children are not learning how to cross a street. Apparently, the increasing anxiety that parents have about their children's safety has led them not to permit children to cross alone, even at ages when that would be quite easy. Excessive supervision is pervasive in every area of parenthood (now unfortunately called "parenting," referring to the technology and skills of parenthood) and has led to parenthood becoming an excessively onerous and burdensome task. Many authorities consider this a most dangerous development, robbing children of the independence and free time they have always needed and creating frustrated and some-times abusive parents.

To provide for the child's mobility, we must build cities with chil-dren in mind and devise transportation systems that work for them. This is no easy task. Mass transit systems are difficult to design and dif-ficult to sell because of our commitment to high-speed automobile travel. This design problem demands wrenching and large-scale changes. It means reducing our use of and reliance on the automobile. It means reorienting our work, play, family life, and commercial activi-ties so that they are all close to each other. Reducing our need for auto-mobiles (or at least for second cars) in this way would deliver the additional benefit of developing stronger communities, more interper-sonal activities, greater involvement, and improved safety on the streets.

One cannot help but think what a much better life we would all have if the automakers had not corruptly undermined the railroad companies almost a century ago. We would be traveling on rails at hun-dreds of miles an hour from the centers of our communities to any-where in comfortable seating, viewing landscapes, walking around, visiting lounges, dining luxuriously in a special car at tables with table-cloths. We wouldn't have the delays, security checks, luggage loss, and tight seats associated with airline travel. Light rail travel would make our automobiles almost unnecessary.

Ahh, but back to reality.

Our devotion to the automobile and our dependency on it has placed the auto in a position of priority over children. Sweden has taken steps to fix that. For example, laws give the same rights to children as to cars when it comes to the assignment of space in the design of new apartment complexes. The United States does not even have these minimal priorities.

Most of the proposed solutions to the problem of safety for children are respectful of the automobile: overpasses and underpasses, crosswalk guards, marked crossings, traffic signals, cul-de-sacs, pedestrian walkways that connect the child's home with school and stores. Some of these solutions are helpful but carry with them their own limitations. Overpasses and underpasses are expensive and cause the additional worry of crime. Crossing guards are helpful, but it is a hazardous duty. Until Americans are using bicycles in great numbers, there will not be adequate provisions to make bicycle travel safe. In new housing developments, pedestrian walkways that permit children to walk to schools and parks without crossing streets seem to be a good solution but in practice bring a number of problems. Because Americans are so committed to building fences and walls to separate themselves from their neighbors to guarantee privacy and the boundaries of their own property, we have transformed what could be beautiful pathways into walled alleys where children are bullied or robbed by other children. Too often, adults have had to be posted in these corridors to supervise so that fights and thefts would not occur, defeating one of the main purposes of the walkway.

Rational efforts to reduce the danger of pedestrian mobility have led to marked crosswalks, traffic signals, and signs, but reliance on rational methods is probably unwise. One look at the statistics would help us realize why these techniques will not work: 39 percent of all pedestrian deaths involve people known to have been drinking; 43 percent are children under the age of four; and 36 percent of the deaths are people over the age of 65. Based on this information, it is clear that almost all pedestrian deaths involve people for whom rational methods, signals, and signs would not be appropriate; they are for one reason or another unable to respond to them. This means that for safe pedestrian travel it will be necessary to people-proof the system, making it impossible for people to walk in front of automobiles. The implication is that we will have to put automobiles where there are no people or put people where there are no automobiles. It certainly isn't going to be resolved by improved driver education. Architect Buckminster Fuller understood the folly of that approach. He held that rather than put more money into driver education, we should design our transportation systems so that people couldn't crash into each other. Design can offer solutions where education cannot. And think what design solutions would do for harried parents and their relationships to their children.

That is not a minor issue because those relationships can create the most deeply troubling issues in the child's world. Children essentially have no options but to live with their parents, no matter what the situation with them might be, and as we all well know, not all parents are good for their children. Children are abused hundreds of thousands and perhaps as many as 4.2 million times a year in the United States, abuse committed almost entirely by parents. In addition to those brutalized, 2,000 are murdered, again mostly by their parents. Incest is disturbingly frequent, usually father/daughter. A group of social workers from Minnesota once told me that in one of their rural counties, 75 percent of the families are affected by incest, usually with the mother's approval "to keep the family together."

Hundreds of thousands of children run away every year. But there are essentially no alternative home environments that can offer lasting quarters for children. So children spend time on the street, a few temporarily in halfway houses for runaways, or they wind up in some kind of jail—and the child has done nothing but try to escape a disastrous environment dominated by inadequate and sometimes brutal parents. We can do better, but it means that we have to take a hard look at how family life really works in our society.

It is unforgivable that these victimized children have no place to count on. Many wind up in the juvenile justice system, which is supposed to serve them well but actually is in some ways worse for them than adult penology. One out of every nine children will go through the juvenile court system before age 18. One out of every six boys. Some are held illegally; many have not committed any kind of crime. Most have done nothing that would be considered a crime if done by an adult— running away, curfew violation, truancy, drinking alcohol, incorrigibility, sexual promiscuity—and none have been given a fair trial with due process of law. Most people believe that the juvenile justice system is more benign than the adult system, when in fact it is more unfair, more cruel, more arbitrary, and more repressive. The brutalization continues.

The argument that children will "grow out of it" is not one I can accept. The idea that some day they will be adults and will then have full use of these facilities, full participation in society, and will be independent of their parents only underscores our attitude that childhood is not important in itself but only as a developmental period for adults-in-training. A person's childhood, however, lasts many years, almost an entire generation. This is a long time to ask them to wait. Even more significant, there always will be millions of children, a third of our population, incapacitated in a world not designed for them. They are missing a great deal. And so are we.

Part IV
Shooting Ourselves in the Foot

If, as I propose, the future of design lies in metadesign—design of design, facilitation of programs that serve not just an elite clientele but reach all of the world's people with shelter and work spaces and living arrangements and experiences that elicit people's best—then we need to reconsider the practices that keep designers from serving the larger public or even considering this critical need. Only then can we realize the potential of design, a potential that is greater at this time than ever before.

The major preparatory task is to gain an increased leadership role in this society, a solidly professional one, enabling designers to enjoy the kind of respect that architects received a century ago. Could it be that practices intended to increase respect for the profession actually lower it? Ironically, that may be true. Judging from anecdotes, respect appears to have been greater before all the measures we will be discussing in this section of the book were instituted.

In what follows, we will examine in some detail the various practices of the design professions that I believe are self-defeating in the effort to gain professional status and leadership power. Although they seem to be directed toward raising standards, they actually lower them, demeaning what was once one of the most admired professions. During my tenure as a member of the AIA Board of Directors, I developed a number of concerns over many accepted practices:

- The perils of protectionism (practices that limit the activities of other design professions and sets us against them)
- The dangers of commoditization (which transforms a profession into a commercial enterprise)
- The counterproductivity of licensing (providing evidence to support George Bernard Shaw's remark that professional societies are conspiracies against the public by keeping the profession small and the fees high)
- The backfiring effects of extrinsic rewards (such as our embarrassing obsession with honors and awards)
- The idea of accreditation (which reduces risk-taking, experimentation, and consequently creativity, and is always out of date)
- The corrupting and dangerous practice of engaging in legitimate bribery (through financial contributions to legislators)
- The ineffectiveness and demeaning nature of mandatory education (an oxymoron)

The Evils of Protectionism

When I joined the AIA board I thought I was fully prepared to find the staff and directors in protectionist mode, guarding the profession from encroachment and lobbying for beneficial legislation. But even I was surprised at how many of the activities in which we engaged involved some form of protectionism. I would like to make a case, if I can, that following that path leads us not toward but away from goals expected of us, goals that are clearly set before us when we consult special outside review committees. These committees and the general public often seem to have higher expectations for the future of the professions than do the professional societies themselves.

Protectionism has backfired over and over again for various groups. For example, labor unions are discovering that tenaciously pursuing only protective strategies becomes a problem in a global economy. Ultimately, protectionism creates the opposite of its intention. It is not an expansive way to lead an organization into the future.

The American Medical Association is a case in point and worth discussing in some detail. Through the past six or seven decades, it has worked hard and spent many millions of dollars linking the term "socialized" with "medicine" in an effort to protect its profession from the specter of a national health program. Along the way, to avoid that frightening scenario, it injudiciously put the insurance companies in charge, and we are all now suffering the pain of that decision with them.

But the consequences of the AMA's approach are more serious than just the administrative discomfort and income reduction that physicians are experiencing. In its determination to protect its turf, the group supported the most reactionary elements in every legislative body, just as long as those legislators were willing to vote to avoid "socializing" medicine. As a consequence, little progressive legislation was enacted that could affect poverty, racism, gun violence, environmental pollution, urban decay, suburban sprawl, and countless other problems that fundamentally determine the health of Americans.

Perhaps the most appalling consequence of the AMA's having followed that path is that nearly 50 million Americans are totally without health insurance, and millions more have inadequate coverage. Consequently, even with all its wealth and advanced medical treatment, the United States rates close to the bottom in every comparative measure of health in developed countries. We are the only developed nation without a national health plan. The outcome of the AMA's protectionism not only eroded the profession's control but also seriously impaired the health of Americans.

The AMA is slowly losing another protectionist battle against the encroachment of other health-oriented disciplines—nurses, chiropractors, clinical psychologists, acupuncturists, nutritionists, etc. Under the pretense that it is concerned only with the health and safety of Americans, the AMA was able to hold off for decades the development of these other professions, again by lobbying and giving money to legislators who would vote against these other professions as they sought professional recognition. But eventually the AMA's hold on the turf weakened as these groups gained strength and their own political clout.

Just as doctors are dependent upon nurses but are also threatened by them when nurses attempt to advance their professional stature, architects are both dependent upon and threatened by interior designers, landscape architects, and God knows how many other new design disciplines that seem to be encroaching on architects' turf. Consequently, much of the energy of the staff and board of the AIA is spent doing what it can to raise barriers to the advancement of other professions, such as preventing interior designers from becoming licensed. All of this has led to lawsuits and injunctions, even while most large architectural offices employ many high-level interior designers and landscape architects and could hardly do without them.

This embarrassing situation continues even though it is clear that the future is going to require more collaboration than competition. If we direct our activities to metadesign issues, we will need many more experienced designers from many fields to collaborate. We should do whatever we can to help them advance. Architecture created this monster through a protectionist stance, and now the other design professions are taking a page from architects' book.

The time may be right for an interdesign conference to end the warfare. I have two thoughts about it. First, perhaps it should not be conducted face-to-face, at least not entirely. At the Western Behavioral Sciences Institute we assembled a task force of top specialists representing the full spectrum of opinion to discuss the abortion issue, but we did it over a five-month period entirely by computer conferencing. By so doing, we avoided the acrimony and polarization that would have been almost inevitable in a face-to-face confrontation, and we produced a document that is surely the best discussion ever held on abortion.

Second, maybe an interdesign conference should include all the other design professions so that the focus would be elevated toward a larger goal of interdesign cooperation across the full range of disciplines. Moving away from any specific fight to higher-order shared goals is a proven strategy of conflict resolution. While the interior design/architecture war is the hottest, the basic problem exists generally. We need to seek higher-order solutions, and maybe a more general conference would make that possible. Fighting with other designers is simply unbecoming. I am encouraged to hear some rumblings that such an effort to develop interdesign communication may be in the works. I have my fingers crossed.

In our design professions' avid protectionism stance, we seem to be following the AMA example. But to my mind, it makes even less sense for us than it does for them. Physicians, unlike architects and designers, control almost all their turf. To get medicine or surgery, one is required to go to a physician. But that is far from true for architects, for example. Most of the building is done without the assistance, let alone the control, of architects. The estimates that I have heard generally range in the one-digit numbers to 25 percent. What must the numbers be in the rest of the world? It would seem that professional design has little turf to protect.

Yet the AIA, as the senior design profession, expends a considerable amount of effort making sure that interior designers, landscape architects, architectural designers, urban planners, and others experience roadblocks in their efforts to professionalize and to expand their spheres of influence. As with the AMA, this is done in the name of protecting the health and safety of Americans! The truth is that the safety of buildings is dictated by codes that everyone, regardless of profession, would have to abide by were they to design a building.

As I look at the list of recipients of the AIA's political action committee's contributions, I see that it supports the same reactionary elements that the AMA supports. Politicians who will vote for architects' particular legislative interests will be supported. Meanwhile, the main thrust of their voting undermines major programs that will eventuate in better planning, better housing, better education, better race relations, better distribution of wealth—all of the concerns that over the long term will positively affect not only the practice of architecture but the comfort and shelter and efficiency and beauty of the lives of Americans. These are the politicians who call for an end to the National Endowment for the Arts and other programs that directly benefit architecture.

Professional societies can discontinue financial contributions to legislators, abolish the financial backing part of the political action committee approach, abandon the effort to secure legislation through buying influence (which is nothing more than legalized bribery), and instead go directly to the body politic with a new vision of the contribution architecture and design can make to our lives. If we can't make our case to the people, how strong a case do we have?

Designers in any discipline could embrace in friendship and collaboration the other design disciplines, encouraging them, assisting them, teaching them, learning from them, working with them. To meet the needs of the 21st century, designers should not be caught squabbling over turf. If architects, for example, are called upon to contribute substantially more to the building in America, they will need all the help they can get.

Professional societies need to be able to support their members in standing for the right thing. All design professions need to be less dominated by their clients. We can help accomplish this if we make sure that the societies themselves stand for the right things in theory and in practice. Organization theorist Peter Drucker gave us a saying about the distinction between management and leadership: "Management is doing things right; leadership is doing the right things."

Moreover, completely new kinds of designers are coming along with whom the current design disciplines will be working closely— software designers, cyberarchitects, information architects, entertainment designers, organization designers, special effects designers, and on and on. Let's let the sunshine in. There may be plenty to do if we collaborate and too little to do if we don't. We have much to gain and little to lose. We don't need to protect the small amount of turf we have. Rather, we need to consider the world our desired territory. I believe our chances of advancing on that territory are better if we find ways of working in concert with all professions who share our aspirations to shape its social and physical design.

The Dangers
of Commoditization

C ommoditization refers to the conversion of what sociologists term a "semi-sacred" service (such as medicine, law, ministry, education, journalism, art, and I would include psychology and design) into a commodity, a marketable product, with packaging, advertising, and market research. Many social critics believe that the rampant commoditization of all we hold dear represents the greatest long-term danger our society faces.

Commoditization of a profession alters the nature of our service. Rather than being motivated by the high-order humanitarian calling fundamental to professions, our work and our innovation become directed toward meeting market-oriented goals, distorting the nature of the service we were educated to deliver.

We see this shift clearly, for example, in the transformation (some would say corruption) of commercial network TV journalism. Several decades ago, when Frank Stanton was president of CBS and Walter Cronkite, Eric Sevareid, and Edward R. Murrow were journalists and commentators, that network was known as the Tiffany of broadcast news. It was regarded as a service of the revered Fourth Estate, a cost center, not a profit center, so was exempt at that time from commoditization.

Then commoditization of the news took over. The networks' competitive search for higher ratings and greater market share completely made over the news into what we now call infotainment. Even Jay

Leno, the host of NBC's "Tonight Show," couldn't help calling attention to the absurdity of his own network's coverage of celebrity-for-hire Paris Hilton. While showing almost continuous 24/7 coverage of her every movement during her June 2007 incarceration brouhaha, including video coverage from a helicopter, MSNBC broke for a total of 12 seconds to announce that the chairman of the Joint Chiefs of Staff had been forced to resign ... then immediately returned to Paris Hilton.

Perhaps a more serious example was the slight coverage given to what was called the 2002 Downing Street Memo, a British memo that came to light in 2005 possibly confirming the "fixing" of intelligence to lead Britain and America into the war with Iraq, potentially an impeachable offense. The three commercial TV networks in the United States devoted a total of six news segments to that coverage. At the same time, these networks devoted 465 news segments to the Michael Jackson trial. That is commoditization.

Even that imbalance doesn't sound so serious until we are reminded that journalism is our main protection against tyranny and other serious threats to our society. President Thomas Jefferson said that if you have to choose between government and the press, take the press. Investigative journalism enables us to have a democracy. Without it we will lose our democratic way of life. And with the exception of publicly supported PBS in the United States and BBC in the United Kingdom, broadcast journalism is all but lost. So commoditization of a profession can have profound effects indeed. Mostly negative, I'm sorry to say.

We have to be reminded again that while commoditization is dangerous, that does not mean we should abandon the market system. A market economy based on competition among purveyors of goods and services for consumer spending is central to the economic and political progress made in the past several hundred years. This competition for the consumer's attention, while sometimes unfair or fraudulent, has led, by and large, to the availability of better services and products and to a rise in the standard of living.

An important distinction needs to be made, however, between the kinds of institutions that do well in a competitive, market-oriented framework and those in which innovation and progress are stunted. Essentially, the difference is between businesses and professions. The market system can exist without democracy, but there has never been a democracy without the market system. So we need both business and professions, and once again we must distinguish between them.

Market orientation tries to satisfy what we might call wants, what people desire or can be made to desire. Professions, on the other hand, are committed to serving needs, the fundamental services that keep both individuals and society healthy and promote positive growth and development.

Wants are manipulated by advertising and marketing. Fashion is a good illustration, but there are innumerable others. Breakfast cereal manufacturers manipulate the wants of wide-eyed children. Automakers inspire otherwise cautious adults to covet SUVs.

But when physicians, for example, advertise to encourage cosmetic surgery, weight loss, or other medical procedures, we enter different territory. That is the reason there are ethical limitations on such advertising in all professions. Unfortunately, those restrictions are loosening or being ignored, and in most professions today there is a dangerous drift toward a competitive market orientation.

In the United States, 16 percent of physicians now have business degrees. If physicians increasingly see their work as a commodity and their patients as consumers and begin to compete to create a market for their special services, we will have a medical system based increasingly on wants rather than needs. To ensure high-quality healthcare, physicians must collaborate, not compete. That essential difference between a profession and a business must be protected.

The professions must be immune, as much as possible, from financial incentives so that they can pursue the goals and values of humanitarian service, which are clearly not those of the private sector. Nor can efficiency, a primary goal in business, be the primary criterion of performance in a profession.

Let's step out of the medical profession and look at the same situation in higher education. University professors have plenty to worry about as they look to the future and so do we all. My friend Farhad Saba is a professor of educational technology at San Diego State University and the former head of educational broadcasting in Iran during the reign of the Shah (which gives him a special sensitivity to the issue of business vs. profession). He recently shared with me a paper that he authored. In one section, he calls attention to the misapplication of the value of efficiency in what he refers to as the industrialization of higher education, a disturbing scenario the National Education Association labels "Warehouse A&M."

He writes, "It enrolls as many students as possible. Students learn on a campus with a population of 100,000. Most of what they experience is automated via technology, and exams are conducted by asking multiple-choice questions, but inefficiency is rewarded because the longer students stay in the institution, the more they pay in tuition fees. To resolve some of these issues the 'education maintenance organization' (EMO) emerges, with which the states and federal government sign a series of agreements to offer educational services to students. In an EMO, contact time with the instructor is set at 15 minutes and all other student encounters with the institution are rationed as well." He asks, "How did a system that is the envy of the world come to look at such an uninviting future?"

The University of Phoenix is a private-sector, for-profit university and is immensely successful financially. When it went public with a stock offering, its founder personally made several hundred million dollars and is now a billionaire. The university is a leader in online distance education, and it also has many campuses that offer classroom experiences. It is a highly efficient system supported almost entirely by tuition income.

Its instructors are essentially drawn from fully employed practitioners. Few are Ph.D.'s. The curriculum is carefully designed by committees, and instructors must follow the plan to the letter. It is a perfect example of private-sector values serving a largely middle-aged, working-class segment of society, a "market" that was previously neglected. It has become the largest university in the country, enrolling more than 350,000 students.

But its way of operating as a business and the values that are implied are quite different from those of traditional colleges and universities in which the organizational design gives faculty freedom to teach as they please and encourages their individual scholarship and research, what we refer to as academic freedom. But academic freedom is sometimes messy. Effective, but not very efficient.

Education is not just determined by curriculum or course title but by the metacommunication sent by the form, design, and organization of the university. This includes the way academic decisions are made, the freedom of inquiry the university encourages, and the independence of thought, originality, and unique individual development it fosters. If these new educational organizations became the model for higher education, there would be a universal erosion of those values, leading to just the opposite of education, leading to uniformity. Because of their academic freedom and other professional values, universities stand as a bulwark against those who would destroy our freedoms and possibly impose autocracy. We need higher education's products, both faculty and students, to be developed as creative, independent, critical thinkers.

Making this distinction, one that honors professional goals over all else, is not a casual matter. It is crucial. Education is not a matter of picking the most efficient delivery system. Much that we prize about our civilization is at risk.

It all seems so innocent. So what if something precious is developed into a marketable commodity, whether it is a person, an idea, or a profession? That seeming innocence, even what seems to make good business sense, may not make such good sense when we get better at making those necessary distinctions. The AMA annually receives $20 million selling the biographies of its members to drug companies so that they can market more effectively to those doctors.

So what if the AMA is commoditizing itself and its members? So what if half of the continuing education of physicians is financed by drug companies? The consequence, I'm here to tell you, is not just corrupting medical practice. It eventually causes the loss of our freedoms. Commoditization is one of the most pernicious and largely invisible developments of our society—far more corrupting of our values than sex and violence on TV, especially because we don't realize it is happening to us.

Designers are continually encouraged by their professional societies not to avoid commoditization but to practice it, to find ways to make their services saleable to the corporate market. Basically, that means offering the market services at a lower price. But why should professional services be offered at a lower price? Why should design firms suffer from the pressure for ever lower pricing? What makes sense in selling widgets does not apply to professional services. If you sell only one widget, it is very costly, but selling thousands makes them cheap. But that reasoning cannot apply to professional service, where top quality is the only acceptable form of service, and the costs remain constant. Efficiency is not and should not be a high value in professional work compared to quality and creativity.

There are other ways to think about dealing with commoditization besides lowering prices. Some firms differentiate their services from the competition, establish trusting relationships with the client, or emphasize quality. These are certainly understandable, and who can be against establishing trusting relationships and emphasizing quality? The issue is why. What is the motivation? If it is only to increase a firm's competitiveness, then the aspects we value most, such as authentic professional relationships, will be commoditized, turned into skills and techniques, soon cheapened and ultimately falsified.

The real problem in commoditization is that it is unprofessional. Professions cannot serve the market, even though it is surely common to put the issue in those terms. Professions must rise above market demands. They must listen and analyze and look at the larger context, conceive the work in terms of what people truly need, and then organize to serve that need. Business, on the other hand, practices a different kind of listening. In business it makes sense to determine what will sell to the market, using focus groups, polling, and other research methods—not to discover what will be good for society but what the market will buy. For a profession, that approach is ultimately self-destructive. On the other hand, research to understand society's needs is in a very different category and leads to very different outcomes.

The other aspect of commoditization that is unprofessional is that it is competitive. It may seem strategically smart to describe one's work in terms of a competitive model, meaning that the task is to beat the competition. But a profession must do just the opposite: It must be collaborative. To progress as a discipline, practice, science, or profession, we must continually collaborate, learn from each other, help each other, and call upon each other when our clientele needs something more or different than we offer. A business can be, must be, competitive. But a profession is in a very different position in society and to serve us well must be goal-oriented, not market-oriented, and collaborative, not competitive.

The Downside of
Honors and Awards

U ntil recently I had never won an award of any kind. So when I began my service in 1999 on the Board of Directors of the AIA in the capacity of public director (non-architect), I was more than a bit nonplussed by the overwhelming attention paid to honors and awards. After all, surgeons, attorneys, professors, judges, and clergy don't have award programs. Why does architecture?

More than 400 pages of the *Almanac of Architecture and Design* are given over to a listing of major awards and fellowships. That doesn't even include the many local award programs. A conversation I had some years ago with prominent architect Stanley Tigerman revealed that he had already collected 110 awards. I wonder how many he has now. The design firm Skidmore, Owings & Merrill has more than 800. The design superstars cannot even accept all they are offered. I found this obsession over awards to be puzzling, amusing, embarrassing, and as a psychologist, somewhat upsetting because I am aware of the research documenting their counterproductivity.

Contrary to what most people believe, giving awards is not a benign activity. The weight of psychological research on this subject shows clearly that extrinsic rewards are ultimately demotivating, not just because there are always a lot more losers than winners, but the pursuit of awards paradoxically distracts people from the work itself. Genuine rewards, the kind that lead to further innovation, are always intrinsic to the process of the work. That's why managers in all kinds of organizations are now trying to make work more interesting rather than thinking up external rewards like trips to Cancun. In both industry and education, countless studies show that honors, awards, prizes, bonuses, A grades, gold stars, even praise, have negative consequences. Performance reviews are in the same category. Practically all evaluations and competitions have been shown to be similarly wrongheaded.

A major real estate developer once told me that he would never hire an award-winning architect. (Could he even find one who has no awards?) He wants the architect to be fully devoted to him and his project, without an eye to winning some prize from the profession. That's why the leading advertising firm Wells Rich Greene will not allow employees to enter award competitions. It distracts them from their clients.

The litany against such award programs is long, beginning with the notorious jinx conferred by the Nobel Prize. Winning that prize virtually guarantees that no work at a comparable level will ever be done again by the winner. I feel lucky that I am in a field that does not offer the Nobel. I was once a guest at a roundtable conference of top scientists gathered at the University of California, Los Angeles. At one point in the discussion I could tell that the group was at an impasse. The scientist sitting next to me leaned over and whispered, "That woman across the table knows the answer to the question that is stopping us now but she won't tell us because she doesn't want any of us to beat her to the Nobel." So much for scientific communication. That's how the Nobel really works.

Now about that award I did win. By surprise I was notified that my co-author and I had won the McKinsey Award for having written what an independent panel judged to be the best article to appear in the *Harvard Business Review* that year. I didn't even know such an award existed. My first reaction was to laugh because the article was about success and failure and included a highly critical analysis of the practice of giving extrinsic rewards of any kind. I figured the judges couldn't resist the delicious irony.

Like many winners of awards, I immediately went to thinking of other reasons of that sort to explain how I might have won it. Since I had a terrific co-author in writer Ralph Keyes, who has written 13 successful books, I imagined having teamed with him might explain it. Then I saw the list of judges and noted that I was acquainted with one of them personally. Well, I thought, maybe that explains it. I'm sure you readers who have won awards understand that process of discrediting oneself because you know enough to have seen how awards are often judged and why they are given. In one ceremony, a prominent design award winner, beset with such feelings, set fire to all of his awards. Another uses a major award as a toilet paper holder. It seems architects collect awards now the way batters number home runs, for their statistical significance.

You probably are aware that awards are less often given to mavericks, to those whose pioneering work really shapes a field, or to women. (Unbelievably, Jane Jacobs was never even nominated for the AIA Gold Medal, and out of 64 winners, none are female.) The politics of awards is an interesting if somewhat appalling field of study. There are no pure honors, not the Nobel, not any. All are confounded with politics, fashion, favoritism, orthodoxy, intrigue, hidden agendas. People get honorary doctorates instead of a fee to give a commencement address, prizes are intended to call attention to the organization more than the honoree, movie studios spend millions to win an Oscar, and so on.

A persuasive case can be made that architectural awards are good advertising for the profession. The award photos certainly do gain a lot of free display space in newspapers and magazines. But I think they also paint a picture of the profession to which most people cannot relate. They cannot imagine that those fabulous homes could ever be theirs, for example.

Award photos rarely identify the profession with solving the most pressing problems of shelter around the world, let alone other contributions architecture can make to reduce a great range of social and human problems. Consequently, the public does not often look to architecture and design for help in those areas. But design can help because it creates situations, not just buildings. And situations, as every psychologist knows, are the most powerful determinants of behavior—

more powerful than anything. That's why I put so much of my hope for the future in the design professions. And that is what the magazine coverage should illustrate.

I was reading the framed certificates on the wall of a chiropractor's office one day, and my mounting nervousness reached a peak when I came to one, at least two-feet square with matting and frame, recognizing his having been elected vice president of his class.

Perhaps the most disturbing aspect of awards is that they seldom are given to people to whom we are indebted for radically reshaping the field. Indeed, those people are ignored or rejected because their ideas challenge prevailing attitudes, undermine practices, force change. Their value is often not recognized in their lifetimes.

Along with others who knew him, I was asked to write a eulogy memorializing the life of the late Victor Papanek, the industrial designer who pioneered the field that now has wide acceptance as universal design—design for the physically or mentally disabled and others socially or politically marginalized. When the journal carrying these many eulogies appeared, practically all of them mentioned how the profession had shunned him for most of his career. Not only was he not honored in those days, but his invitation to be a speaker at a national meeting was actually withdrawn because of his critical attacks on the profession for ignoring this disadvantaged population and devoting itself instead to cosmetic design and currying the favor of white middle-class clients.

There will be no awards for the mavericks, the radicals, the profound innovators, the critics, the outsiders, just as there weren't for Darwin, Freud, Gandhi, and Einstein at the time they did their masterworks. Indeed, receiving an award from your profession means you are safely in the mainstream. I should remind you that Frank Lloyd Wright and Buckminster Fuller were in their 80s by the time the AIA got around to awarding them the Gold Medal. The innovators are often not appreciated.

In conversations with architects, I have found that I am not alone in my opposition to honors and awards. Many are embarrassed, as I am, by the self-congratulatory nature of awards and the time they take out of what could otherwise be productive meetings. I recall my experience as a keynote speaker at the 1998 AIA convention in San Francisco. The plenary session in which my talk was presumably the main event was scheduled to start at 9:15 a.m. and be an hour and a half long, ending with my 45-minute speech, and "only a few awards to give first," I was told. I was to be finished with my talk at 10:45. After all the awards had been given out, I was introduced at 10:40. I began with, "Any questions?"

Awards are the enemy of innovation. If you want to delve into the negative effects of extrinsic rewards, there is a marvelous book by Alfie Kohn, *Punished by Rewards*, which summarizes the literature and makes the case compellingly. And as we all know, the major innovations in any field are greeted with just the opposite of awards. They are first ridiculed, then treated with hostility, followed eventually by grudging acceptance.

While we are in the neighborhood, let's look at fellowships, of which there are thousands in any design profession. I am not a fellow of the American Psychological Association because these days one must apply for a fellowship, and somehow applying for an honor seems, well, odd to me. In the old days, some senior group would identify a few of the major figures in a field and they would be tapped for fellowship. But fellowship no longer means that you are a top psychologist, nor does it mean you are a top designer. Top designers are often fellows, but mostly it means you have rendered some kind of a service to the profession, which could mean that you held some office in the association. I find the whole fellowship business not contributing to respect for design at all because there are so many thousands of fellows that both insiders and many outsiders know perfectly well are not necessarily the best designers. What does that do for the profession?

These award programs did not exist when architecture was in full flower. What? Architects were once more influential than they are now? Indeed they were. Architects do not have the leadership status they once did when they were deeply involved in the high councils of decision making, creating institutions like the Union League Club, fighting slavery and advocating other social causes, associating with presidents. Architect and U.S. Ambassador Richard Swett has documented that history in his book, *Leadership by Design*. If architects are to enjoy that position again, one that would permit them to influence the future of design greatly, they need to regain that lost respect.

Later in this book, in the section on leadership, we will look at the role of success and failure in some detail and how poorly those terms are understood. Let me just say here, as we question the practice of rewarding with honors and prizes, if you want to stimulate innovation and the necessary risk-taking it requires, treat success and failure the same way—not with rewards or punishment, not even with evaluation, but by understanding and engagement, regarding every well-intended failure as just another step on the road to achievement.

But what about losing the quasi-advertising function of awards? Not to worry. First of all, a building does not have to be award-winning to be interesting or to be displayed in a magazine. But there are bigger fish to fry. Architecture and the other design professions should be planning in the trillions of dollars. Just showing beautiful buildings or dramatic interiors or glamorous illustrations does not serve to educate the public on what could be design's most important and most remunerative calling—its power to address the major problems of homelessness, slums, crime, illness, and ethnic conflict that so cripple our global society and to foster the creativity, cooperation, and affection necessary to help build a better world—a world I believe design can make possible. But seeing photos of rich people's award-winning homes may be counterproductive in that quest.

More Wrong Turns:
Licensing, Accreditation,
and Mandatory Education

One would think that nothing could guarantee respect for professionals more than knowing they were strenuously tested before becoming licensed and that laws exist making it a crime for others to offer services covered by those licenses. But I don't believe it actually works that way. Indeed, it may have just the opposite effect, lessening public respect.

Early in my career, only two years out of graduate school, I was invited to become a member of the first licensing board in the country for psychologists, in San Diego, Calif. I'm afraid that serving on that board permanently tainted my perception of professionalism. Far from protecting the public, my colleagues and I forced out of business a number of people who, though without credentials, were probably self-taught, well meaning, harmless, and certainly less expensive. I resigned that position.

Years passed, and certification and then licensing of psychologists became national, and it remains strongly in place. But I have always appreciated the irony that in those days the only psychologist ever to lose a malpractice suit was, at the time, chairman of the Psychology Examining Committee for California! So much for protecting the public. For the most part, the dangers to the public come from inside the professions.

I am uneasy about defining myself as a licensed psychologist. I don't take any pride in it. I actually think I'm much better than that.

Licensing sets a minimum standard, but who wants to be there? I would never refer anyone to just a licensed psychologist, and I'm sure you wouldn't refer anyone to just a licensed designer.

I am not suggesting that credentials don't matter. In one's search for a good designer or physician or lawyer, one usually asks around, and beyond that, it can help to know where the potential designer or surgeon or attorney went to school and how he or she is regarded by others in that practice through the recognition of competence bestowed by board certifications, diplomas, etc. But there is an important difference between certification and licensing. Certification simply testifies to one's competence. Licensing actually restricts the practice only to those who pass the tests and doesn't permit anyone else to use the title.

My friend Jim Cramer, former CEO of the AIA, energetically disagrees with me on the issue of licensure of architects, arguing that it is a necessity for the health, safety, and welfare of the public (much as the AMA has argued on behalf of physicians, and look at what that has done for the health of Americans). I think it has proven to be counterproductive to limit the use of the title "architect." People who decide to refer to themselves as scientists, artists, ministers, professors, teachers, and writers, even though they may be inexperienced, are not a threat to the people who are the real thing. It never occurs to any of the latter that they need to protect that title. I think psychologists were more respected when anyone could use the term "psychologist," and I'll bet architects were too.

George Bernard Shaw made the famous remark, "All professions are conspiracies against the laity." He meant that instead of protecting the public, professions do just the opposite, keeping themselves small and expensive. Licensing doesn't protect the public. My experience on the psychology licensing board brought home to me this travesty. By our actions, troubled people were cut off from potentially helpful and inexpensive resources.

It's worth mentioning here that some of the best architects haven't been licensed—Frank Lloyd Wright, Buckminster Fuller—and some of the worst have been—no names here, but I'm sure you have your favorites. The former head of the California Architecture Licensing

Board told me that he no longer believes in licensing, that it does not guarantee competency.

The profession of architecture (and the other design professions are following suit) has made licensing such a lengthy ordeal that many graduates, even some of the best, have no intention of becoming licensed. When I joined the AIA board, I was told that only about 50 percent of architecture graduates planned to seek licenses. Two years later, when I went off the board, it had dropped to 30 percent. Recently an outstanding architecture senior, who had decided to become a kindergarten teacher, told me her private study of those intending to apply indicated the number was more like 12 percent.

Think about it. Does the public need to be protected against people who practice architecture? What does that say?

And what of accreditation? As a former dean of a design school, I can testify to the dampening effect of accreditation. This effect, by the way, is usually not because the visiting accreditation committee has deliberately stifled creative educational processes. Indeed, most individual committee members encourage innovation even if their guidelines don't always foster it. Sometimes, the actions of the committee do shut down plans or ventures that have been important to the faculty and deans, but more often it is the total process itself, the whole idea of accreditation. So much depends upon getting accreditation—status and funding for the school, student loans, recognition for licensing, etc. that one cannot risk failing. So the real stifling comes before the committee even arrives. It is in the self-censorship that occurs in the preparation of the report to the committee.

One of the most difficult problems with accreditation is the serious lag time. Guidelines are by definition out of date the minute they are approved. Accreditation committees cannot possibly be on the leading edge, and it takes years to remove criteria that have truly expired. Traditional libraries were required long after libraries could be accessed online.

The accrediting process is justified because we have bought into the ideas of standards, of evaluation, of grading, and of basic skills, none of which foster innovation or better educational experiences. Evaluation, for example, is for management, not for learning. And we continually find that basic skills are sometimes antiquated but also perhaps not even basic. Just as musicians, some of the greatest, often cannot read music, so it is with design. The icon of contemporary architecture, Frank Gehry, would be lost if he were to have to perform the computer skills necessary to achieve his designs.

I am not the only dean to have found myself dreading accreditation. I spoke recently with the dean of a major school of architecture, someone I greatly admire, who was livid over the treatment his school received by the accreditation committee. Believe me, that is not uncommon. Accreditation is a deadly process. It stifles innovation, the most important fundamental in educational design. It should be abandoned.

To complete my list of activities of the design professions that fail to win the respect they are presumably intended to achieve, let's look at mandated education—an oxymoron if there ever was one. Mandated education is the requirement that in order to continue professional practice one must regularly take a certain number of continuing education courses in that field. I won't spend time on the philosophy of education on which this practice is based, if indeed there is such a philosophical base, which I doubt. I would assume that any group interested in pedagogy leading to significant learning would not think it the wisest. Moreover, you might be surprised to learn what qualifies as continuing education. When I was on the board of the AIA we held a meeting at the Air Force Academy in Colorado Springs, Colo. During our visit we were taken on a brief tour of the facility, and one of our members wanted to qualify that as counting toward the fulfillment of his educational obligation. Well, I guess it was educational.

At another meeting, one of the directors reported that a California study had shown that mandated education in architecture had not resulted in improvement of practice. But the board completely ignored that piece of information and turned to other business. The AIA sponsors many of the continuing educational offerings, so it has become an important source of revenue.

Personally, I would expect good designers to continue learning one way or another, but I am not reassured to know that they have to do that to keep their licenses. It is a corrupt practice in every profession. An article in the *New York Times* about medical education (which is mandated to keep one's license) showed that half of the continuing medical education is designed by and paid for by the pharmaceutical companies, which partly explains why physicians keep prescribing drugs that are known to be dangerous.

Think about it. As with the metamessage of licensing, doesn't the public have reason to worry about the competence of designers who apparently will continue learning only if it is mandated under threat of losing their licenses?

In 2007 the Bush administration decided that every member of its staff with a security clearance would have to take a mandatory ethics course. Does that announcement raise or lower our confidence in their practices?

Part V
Leadership and Management

I f metadesigners are going to realize their potential in serving the public interest, they are going to have to become effective, influential, compassionate leaders. This is not usually built into the education of designers, most of whom expect to be working for a leader rather than becoming one.

This section does not pretend to make anyone a leader. I regard it as outrageous that management and leadership are sometimes made to seem as if they are as easy as reading a book or attending a weekend seminar or motivational lecture. This book will not treat it so simplistically. What I am trying to do is present a picture of what it means for a designer to become a leader, what the designer brings to the party, and what kinds of surprises in the form of paradoxes and absurdities lie ahead. I hope that some of the lessons I have learned will help equip the designer to experience the transition to leader as an adventure rather than an ordeal.

I earlier quoted Peter Drucker who said, "Management is doing things right; leadership is doing the right things." The designer will need to do both, so this section deals with both.

Designers as Leaders

D esign is one of the few professions dominated by its clientele. Compared to physicians, attorneys, and academics, designers are inclined to do what they're told. That posture is so widely accepted among designers that it sometimes seems the only ones who can occasionally insist on having things their way are the superstars of design.

Of course, having one's way is hardly the ideal manner in which to conduct a professional relationship. Nevertheless, design judgment, even in matters of social responsibility such as health and safety, let alone matters of aesthetics, efficiency, productivity, and visual impact, is often subordinated to the client's or employer's wishes.

That is such an old story among designers that perhaps it is small wonder that designers tend not to see themselves as leaders. If they have learned not to expect their professional judgments to sway clients or employers, how can they imagine leading corporations or communities, to say nothing of exercising leadership in the developing global arena? It is simply impossible for most designers to think of themselves as having a place in high councils of decision making.

But that is where designers are most needed—at the top. It is a travesty that the only professionals close to CEOs are lawyers and accountants. Designers have more to offer because increasingly our organizations need to be design-driven, not just market-driven. To truly prosper, global society must have its needs met, not just its wants.

Instead, designers who work in organizations worry about not being appreciated, worry that their work is not understood by top management. As a result, they spend an inordinate amount of time trying to educate the CEO about the benefits of design consciousness, not realizing that every other department is also trying to educate the CEO about the potential contribution it could make because its members feel similarly misunderstood and unappreciated.

The truth is that CEOs don't understand any of the professions or groups represented in the organization and never will. Because things change so fast, they don't even understand the departments they came from. They have other concerns. They have to see the big picture. Most of their time is spent on matters having nothing to do with the internal operations of the organizations they head. Instead, they deal with industry-wide issues, government relations, community needs, raising capital, and so on.

The better strategy for designers would be to regard the current effort to educate the CEO about how designers see the world as a lost cause and instead try to educate themselves about how the CEO sees the world. Is it possible for designers to try to gain that top leadership perspective? If and when they do, they can become the indispensable people occupying chairs at the directors table.

Designers, however, are understandably reluctant to leave their drawing boards or computers, preferring hands-on work with their design problems. Leading, making it possible for others to work with those design problems, somehow seems non-creative, not what they were trained to do. Nevertheless, that is the necessary change designers are going to be called upon to make. If design will be the byword of the 21st century, designers will have to take their places as its leaders.

The fact that it is a difficult change to make shouldn't deter design professionals who have already made many fundamental changes. In recent years, many designers have become cyber designers working in electronic space, metadesigners helping laymen create their own designs, entertainment designers who never expected to be designing experiences rather than things, and so forth. The change to a leadership posture shouldn't be more difficult.

A coroner I know was once asked, "Whatever made you want to

become a coroner?" He thought for a moment and replied, "I don't know … I guess I just like people." That remark is amusing because we often hear people justifying their decisions to take a job or enter a profession with those words, and we tend to regard that motivation as rather superficial. It turns out, however, that when it comes to leadership, it isn't at all superficial. Liking the people one is leading is crucial to success.

Liking people depends not only on the personality and background of the individual but even more on the role relationships one has on the job. Certain professions are engaged in work that risks eroding their respect and liking for people. This may be a work hazard for police, journalists, and lawyers, for example, who often work with people who are misbehaving and deceitful. Other professions—psychologists, for example—tend to create relationships in which their liking and respect for their clients grow.

Where does design stand in this respect? It all depends. When we see people only at their defensive or deceptive worst or when we feel victimized by them, we tend to like them less and less. When designers become lackeys or victims, they will dislike their bosses or victimizers. On the other hand, when they feel they are genuinely helping their clients or employers, they will like them more. We tend to like not the people who do things for us but the ones we do things for. That explains why the best leaders are those who serve the group. Paradoxically, it is more important for leaders to like their people than for their people to like them. Eventually it will be reciprocal.

Many years ago my friend, the late designer George Nelson, told me a story I will never forget. Early in his career, Nelson worked for a time with Frank Lloyd Wright. One day when Nelson and the great prairie architect were taking a walk and talking, Wright was struggling to find a metaphor that would explain the essence of architecture. At one point he stopped and pointed to a flower, saying, "Architecture is like this flower … no, that's not it." He then walked a bit farther, turned and said, "George, architecture is like being in love." After he told me that story, Nelson said, "Dick, I hope it doesn't take you as long as it took me to figure out what he meant by that."

Well, I'm afraid it did. But I'm beginning to get the idea. It is a paradox. In order to be a professional, one must be an amateur. The word amateur comes from the Latin *amator*, meaning to love. Amateur doesn't mean doing something badly but doing it for the love of it. Of course. Love and passion are the organizing forces in leadership and management, overriding technique or skill, just as they are in almost everything that is worthwhile—romance, parenthood, creativity. Paraphrasing Wright—leadership, then, is like being in love. And paraphrasing Nelson—I hope it will not take you as long to understand that as it took me.

Leadership is like being a good host at a dinner party. Consider what that entails. A good host thoughtfully plans the evening, carefully composes the group, takes pains to create the proper environment, arranges the appropriate seating, sets the agenda for the evening, introduces subject matter for discussion, lubricates difficult situations, soothes relationships, takes responsibility, moves things along, attends to details, keeps controversy at a manageable level, adds humor and optimism, comes early and stays late, brings guests into the conversation who previously may have been marginal, handles one thing after another, shifts attention easily, listens well, doesn't dominate, is at ease with self and others, and most important, enables the guests to be at their best.

Leadership is not a skill. There are no expert leaders, just as there are no expert friends or husbands or parents. The more important a relationship, the less skill matters. Leadership is a high art. It is too important to be a skill. It needs to be understood and appreciated for its aesthetic qualities, for its gracefulness and beauty, just as we appreciate these qualities in a great athlete quite apart from that athlete's contribution to the victory. While we can appreciate them in their own right in both sport and leadership, these aesthetic qualities are fundamental to success.

All this must make it seem that becoming a leader is a rather tall order. But there is good news. You already know how. One of the amazing facts about leadership and management is that you can take people right off the production line and make them managers. Without an hour of training they start right in, and the great majority succeed. That's not because the job is easy. In fact, leadership is the most complex, difficult, responsible job our society offers. It makes brain surgery look easy. The reason that brand new managers can do it is that they already know how.

We all have a mastery of roles that we seldom if ever get a chance to play. That new manager has experienced leadership in so many situations in life that he or she has unconsciously acquired the role and only needed the right situation for the right behavior to be elicited.

Designers have even better preparation than most to assume leadership. They are especially qualified. Designers are already good at seeing things in context, already understand the sweep of history, are already conversant in the arts, sciences, and humanities (as are the best leaders), are already good at working in ensembles, are already environmentally aware, are already aware of the limits of technology and its backfiring nature, are already capable of a high level of creative thinking, are already appreciative of the aesthetic dimensions of leadership. The first step, then, is for designers to begin to imagine themselves as leaders—of design firms, of communities, of cultural organizations, of corporations, and beyond.

This century will probably determine the survival of our civilization. We will succeed only if design becomes the organizing discipline of the future, and that will happen only when designers become leaders. The world needs what designers have to offer—not just on the drawing board but on the board of directors.

18

The Changing Game of Leadership

T here was a time, not so long ago, when leaders felt they could succeed by observing what were regarded as the principles of management, for example, "Praise in public, reprimand in private" and "The span of control of a manager should not exceed five people." Not only have such principles been largely discredited (praise has been shown not to be a motivator, and as organizations have flattened the hierarchy of their organization charts, many more people can be included in that span of control), but the idea that one could rely on simplistic principles in an infinitely complicated and dynamic situation now seems quaint.

The game has changed. Most leaders today recognize the importance of the recent developments in our economy and in our institutions that have dramatically altered our ways of doing business: the growth of service industries and financial institutions, the creation of global organizations and markets, the shift to a knowledge-based economy, and the explosion of new technologies, particularly new communication technologies. Less well understood is that these developments demand very different ways of leading and managing. Indeed, they require a revolution in thinking about the fundamental concepts of leadership.

As we enter the era in which protectionism must give way to collaboration, competition is combined with alliances, change is constant, profitable programs must be scrapped to make room for new business, and accelerated innovation is demanded, the old bromides and out-dated management principles don't work. The day is over when leadership development could be thought of as skill training or that management change could be accomplished by a motivational pep talk or a pop psychology book.

Just when managers thought they had a skilled approach to handling organizational problems through gaining listening and negotiating skills or new techniques of re-engineering or benchmarking or accountability, the requirements shifted. Indeed, the new demands come at managers so rapidly now that for all practical purposes, the need to adapt is constant. That adaptation is made even more difficult because of its increasing complexity.

This means that leaders must be able to transcend fads. (Remember quality circles, total quality management, zero defects, management by objective, Six Sigma?) Instead of acquiring specific skills and techniques, which are never enough to deal with the extraordinary complexities and challenges of organizational life, leaders must develop a posture based on critical thinking, trust their intuitions, understand the paradoxical nature of human affairs, see the larger picture, and possess that uncommon quality, common sense. In short, they must be able to exercise the one characteristic that is the basis of all effective leadership—wisdom.

Management is becoming a true profession. Managers can no more function in this new world by reading simplistic advice books than can physicians or lawyers or architects. Leadership and management, whether in the context of a corporation, an educational system, a hospital, or a design firm, have always been far more complicated than they seem, and those complications have mounted. The situations managers face are actually more complex than those faced by these other professions because managers are dealing not only with the exigencies of individuals but also of organizations and, even more convoluted, of social and political systems.

None of the qualities associated with leadership—vision, perspective, courage, optimism, decisiveness, tenacity, wisdom, and compassion—can be learned as skills. But they can be learned through education, dialogue, or reading—where the leader's experience is wedded to important ideas. That is, managers need rich opportunities to examine their experience in the light of new research and new concepts, and they must be prepared to alter their fundamental assumptions about how human affairs work.

The good news is that by and large, their experiences in work and in life have already given them much that they need for a management role. But that role needs constant attention. It needs to be nurtured, encouraged, released, and fine-tuned to meet current requirements.

Designers already have the most important requirement, the one that most leaders and managers do not think about. They are already designers of situations, environments, organizations, relationships, and experiences. Design is the rubric of the future, not just in management but in every field because it is such a powerful determinant of human behavior and experience.

What are these other new requirements? What does this decade, this year, this week call for? How can the manager meet the challenges of constant innovation and change, the acquisition of new technologies, the collapse of trust in government and corporations, the conflicting demands of globalization, the contradictions of geopolitics? What would characterize a posture that could address those challenges? What does today's manager need to think about?

First, the paradoxical nature of human affairs. Behavior is seldom rational. That is why so much of it seems absurd. The leader who understands this and can practice paradoxical management is going to be a step ahead. In human affairs, paradox is the rule, not the exception; therefore, leadership is essentially the management of dilemma.

Second, the necessary conditions for achieving innovation. Even in risk-averse times, such as the current economic climate, the need for innovation continues even with respect to inventing better management systems to cope with such difficulties because innovation in every area is vital not just for a positive bottom line but for continued professional achievement.

Third, an understanding of the true nature of success and failure—their confusing consequences, their similarity, their interdependence, the management case for increasing risk-taking and its inevitable failures, and the need to treat both success and failure the same way, as steps to further achievement. When one's outdated concept of success and failure changes, everything else about management changes too. We need to drop the terms "success" and "failure" from the lexicon of leadership and management.

Fourth, an understanding of the changing work force—the conditions that motivate or fail to motivate employees, the different orientation of the younger generation, the questionable role of morale, the unorthodox working arrangements in high-tech corporations, the difference between intrinsic and extrinsic rewards, the importance of personal engagement.

Fifth, an appreciation of the new context of work. The working environment is increasingly nongeographic, global, electronic, digital, and highly communicative. Virtual management is simply different in ways that profoundly affect innovation and productivity. Working in the information-based organization, as all are now, calls for fundamentally different attitudes and understanding about hierarchy and organization design, collaboration at a distance, distributed leadership, working in isolation, developing community, involving previously marginal employees, and what constitutes effective online communication.

Sixth, a commitment to a new ethics of leadership. To regain the trust necessary for public support, even internal support, today's leaders must examine and revise the fundamental philosophies that guide their actions and underlie every management decision. The disturbing recent events with major corporations and institutions, including government, have made it impossible for leaders to take their reputations for ethical behavior for granted.

Seventh, the development of a courageous vision, which may be the most important of all leadership qualities. Courageous vision comes from transcending the conventional to imagine unprecedented events along a time horizon as much as decades in the future. It is a product not of predicting the future, which is impossible, but of attending to the big picture, understanding larger forces, trends, and cycles, increasing a sensitivity to social, political, and technological changes, releasing the playfulness to dream and developing the courage to act.

All of these new qualities, these new learnings, combine to form the qualities needed by metadesigners. Together they help managers at all levels acquire a stronger posture, one that is nimble yet rooted in more sophisticated ways of thinking about the management of human affairs. Gaining these understandings, developing this wisdom, can come only from integrating the personal experience of the manager with powerful ideas about how people actually behave and how organizations can be made to work. That is the new task of leadership development. These are the messages that leaders need to hear now to open their minds to the new ways they must operate in the very different organizational climate of the 21st century.

Leadership Is
Not About Skills

mericans tend to believe that getting along in life is a matter of acquiring skills. However unwarranted that belief may be, we continue to reduce even the most complex situations, including the personal and intimate ones such as parenthood and love making, to the level of skills and techniques. Now leadership, that most mysterious and fascinating human endeavor, is increasingly the subject of skill training.

While we refer constantly to "leadership skills" and have been exposed to countless books and courses dealing with that subject, the truth is that leadership is not a matter of skill. That is, there are no expert leaders. There are good leaders, even great leaders, but they are not expert because neither we nor they know how they developed that ability.

The role of leader is far too important to be accomplished by skills. As I have emphasized before, the more important a relationship, the less skill matters. There are no friendship skills, husband skills, romantic skills. Indeed, it would seem rather inappropriate, actually quite wrong, to demean those precious relationships by reducing them to sets of skills. Leadership, too, deserves more respect than to be demeaned by skill training.

If not skills, what are the qualities that characterize good leadership? Most organization researchers agree that successful leaders demonstrate vision, courage, optimism, integrity, perspective, openness, concentration, presence of mind, intuition, wisdom, compassion, and extraordinary commitment to organizational goals. How could we ever have thought these qualities could be achieved by skill training?

Indeed, skill training in human relations can even be counterproductive. I realize that statement is close to heresy. Given the millions of human relations training programs that companies sponsor and having myself introduced the term "active listening" into the lexicon of human relations skill training, my comment demands explanation.

To begin, it is important to distinguish between training and education. Training is highly useful in learning such skills as language acquisition, computer programming, and budgeting, where it is desirable for people to learn the same skills, to become more alike, as it were. Education is just the opposite. When education is successful, people become different from each other because they have combined an exposure to important ideas with their own significant experiences to form a uniquely individualized posture toward life and work.

The trouble comes when we fail to realize that training and education differ radically in both process and outcomes. Training leads to skills, which inevitably lead to a new sense of responsibility and expectation about one's ability to handle the area in which the skill is to be applied. But since skills are seldom sufficient to match the complexity of the situation, they lead to frustration and a new sense of powerlessness. Feelings of responsibility in human relations coupled with feelings of powerlessness represent a dangerous combination, often leading to abuse. That is why doctors who cannot cure their patients or teachers whose students do not learn or parents who cannot control their children do not become compassionate. They are more likely to become abusive.

Education, on the other hand, leads to a very different outcome. It first leads to information, then to knowledge, then to understanding, and, in the right hands, to wisdom. The inevitable consequence of wisdom is humility, which is the basis for compassion, the *sine qua non* of leadership.

What then should constitute the education of leaders? Apparently not business alone. Only a small percentage of CEOs have MBAs. Many of our best corporate and government leaders are grounded in the humanities. Exploring the great ideas and events of history, appreciating the arts and cultures of the world, understanding the basics of scientific and philosophical inquiry, delving into the deeper meanings of literature—what we call a liberal education—these have shaped their judgments, decisions, and actions in fundamental, salutary ways even though the particular influences of any specific course cannot be known.

If not skills, what then can we offer designers in the way of a leadership development program? The ideal curriculum can and certainly should be debated continually. Let me suggest three areas of learning I would include.

Context. To be able to take the long view, metadesigners need an understanding of the larger context in which their decisions are imbedded. They need knowledge of the sweep of history that has created the present, the importance of resource management and environmental issues, of community relations, of the possibilities, limits, and unintended consequences of technology, of demographics and the changing nature of the work force, of the relationship of corporations and government, of capital and productivity, of geopolitics and political economy, of globalism and interdependence.

Assumptions. To be able to act freely, with presence of mind and with an openness to new ideas, it is important that metadesign leaders develop new ways of thinking, unencumbered by deeply held stereotypes, ideologies, and belief systems that narrow one's perspective. To accomplish this they need to examine the philosophical, ethical, and cultural assumptions they may not even know that they hold.

People. To be able to lead and inspire, executives need to know about people—about themselves and others as leaders and members of groups, about the interpersonal underworld, about the paradoxical nature of human affairs. This knowledge is gained not just to change people, who are usually pretty good the way they are, but rather to understand them because understanding is the basis for the creation of community, the first responsibility of leadership. To build community, leaders need to be able to make more accurate assessments of the human resources at their disposal and even more important, to be able to develop, through new ways of being, the respect and caring that create fellowship.

Isn't that a rather tall order? Of course. But the need is great, as is the payoff. Leadership, after all, is the most powerful and vital force on earth. Nothing is more important than executives coming to understand the constantly changing requirements of leadership. We have to say farewell to the days when executives could operate on the basis of a few stable management principles and put behind us the idea that leaders can be trained. But leaders can be educated. The increasing complexity of the situations in which executives now find themselves, however, demands that leadership education be profound, intensive, and continuous throughout their careers. Fortunately, we now have the advanced computer communication technology that makes such continuing education of leaders possible.

Paradoxically, those who seem to need this education least, who are already ahead of the game, are the ones who can profit most. The better the leaders, the more they can grow and change from exposure to new ideas. Too often we see such educational programs as remedial, offered only to those who need them most. But the better payoff is in making sure they are offered to the very leaders who don't seem to need them at all. They are the ones who can sprint ahead.

Designers as Managers

The broad ranging discipline of design, with centuries of history, brings an added stature to management, transforming it into more of a true profession. It protects the designer from succumbing to the dominant management approaches of the past few decades—approaches that at first seem to work but over time, don't. Performance reviews, extrinsic incentives, accountability pressures, motivational pep talks, and leadership skill training are all discredited, as are the simplistic management fads that continue to seduce executives and then disappoint them. Design, because it represents not a technique but a more fundamental posture, looms as a powerful alternative.

Nevertheless, the understandable insecurity that comes from taking on what is surely the most complex role in society, that of leadership, may make designers vulnerable to simplistic bromides (like new parents, who have had imposed upon them one of the most complex and difficult roles). Paradoxically, the more complicated the role, the more simplistically society treats it.

Bringing some of the perspectives garnered from the disciplined field of design would help the designer develop a more professional management stance, less buffeted by fads. Professionals such as physicians, lawyers, professors, and architects are far less likely to be entranced by trends and fashion because they have a strong professional perspective that guides them through the challenges.

Designers given leadership roles will begin working with individual employees one-on-one but will soon begin dealing with constellations of people, such as project teams. From there, it is natural for designers to think about the greater context. These small groups are embedded in larger systems—organizations, corporations, and communities. They, in turn, are part of even larger social, cultural, political, and physical systems—industries, cities, and international systems. As they look more intensively at these environments that are so determining of human events, the distinction between social and physical systems blurs. They are interdependent. Each has something important to contribute to the other. That ability to expand one's view and appreciate the forces at work in the larger context is what characterizes a design perspective.

Designers are no strangers to serving organizational life. In addition to creating buildings, they have established corporate identity programs, made open office arrangements, employed color schemes or background music, produced ergonomically correct products, and the like. Few leaders at the top, however, have seen the incorporation of design as central to their management of human relations.

There are exceptions. One is top management's early recognition of the oppressive problems of scale—coping with the overwhelming numbers of people they manage. When eliciting creativity has been crucial, executives have redesigned their huge organizations to create smaller, semi-autonomous units, such as Lockheed's famous Skunk Works, where the stealth fighter was developed, or Xerox PARC, the research center in Palo Alto, Calif., responsible for many advances in computer technology.

Other examples exist where leaders rely on altering form to improve organizational function. They take a project team or a board of directors to a resort for an intensive, uninterrupted meeting on long-term strategic issues. They establish a ground rule in brainstorming that no judgmental comments can be made so as not to shut down further development of an idea. They flatten an organization chart to eliminate unnecessary reporting levels or they redesign the hierarchical structure based on the abilities of managers to deal with increasingly long time horizons. All these actions qualify as social architecture.

Because changing situations is much easier than changing individuals, designers think first of the structural issues in eliciting desired behavior. Rather than starting with the most difficult way of operating (working with the differing personalities and proclivities of people), they start with the larger environment and work back, if necessary dealing with the more stubborn personality issues last.

Those leaders with a bent for social architecture ask, *How can I arrange this work space to be more encouraging of high performance? How can I restructure this group into subgroups that will elicit more innovation? How can I establish ground rules for the kinds of meetings and other interactions we have that will make us more efficient? How can I design a communication system that will facilitate collaboration among far-flung units, creating nongeographic communities? How can I design this situation so that my most creative but most irritable staff member is less likely to be troubled by and trouble for associates? How can I organize our team and workflow so that they are aligned with our goals? How can I design a system that gets people the information they need at just the time they need it without having to work through their supervisors or go to another building for the necessary document? How can I design our organization so that it more closely coincides with the actual patterns of interpersonal trust that exist?*

Designers have to be cautious. More than one organization has moved into newly designed quarters only to discover that the new designs fail to provide for the kind of human interaction the participants had come to depend upon. Business author Fran Hawthorne cites the design of pharmaceutical giant Merck's new headquarters as contributing to its current difficulties in getting new products approved. When all the research, manufacturing, and executive offices were in one place, people interacted more, walked around, and ate in the same cafeteria. The CEO would sit at lunch and talk with anyone, blue-collar workers or scientists, increasing cross-fertilization. "When they moved," she says, "they lost some of the water cooler talk."

As we discussed earlier, leadership is like being a good host. The same is true of managers who identify with a social design approach. They try to arrange the circumstances in which their people can be at their best.

Social design in management embodies a perspective that looks first at the larger context of work and then attempts to make structural arrangements that are conducive to the kind of relationships and behaviors that help meet the overall goals.

Curiously, we often use the aesthetic term "graceful" to describe hosting behavior, but we seldom use such a term to describe leadership and management. Yet when leadership is at its best we witness a special kind of beauty, sometimes earthy, sometimes elegant, but in its own way, aesthetically powerful. The aesthetics of leadership are effective at an unconscious level, surely the most important level, but are largely ignored in management discussions, probably because of management's masculine image. Design, however, recognizes no such constraint. To the contrary, it is built on a primary interest in aesthetics. Embracing a management by design approach, therefore, legitimizes our appreciation of management along these important aesthetic dimensions. Great leaders, like great bullfighters and great athletes, combine form and grace and courage into actions that can only be described as beautiful.

Systems Thinking as Metadesign

E ver since the 1940s, when sociologist William Foote Whyte conducted his famous study of the interpersonal tensions that arise
at peak hours in restaurants, managers have been encouraged to
think about human relations in systems terms. Noticing waitresses
shouting orders to male cooks, Whyte surmised that such behavior vio-
lated role expectations of both gender and status, cooks being of higher
status, and women expected to be subservient to men. (Remember, this
was the '40s.) He designed a system in which the waitress would write
down the order on a small pad of paper and stick the slip of paper on
which she had written the order on a spindle. The cook would then
take it off when he saw fit, calling the waitress when the order was
ready. That system of realigning the roles remains in place, although the
spindle has largely been replaced by a revolving drum or a computer. It
is considered one of the first uses of system design in the management
of human relations in industry.

Since then, the technology of systems design of operations and
workflow, aided by software design and information technology, has
had many advocates and made innumerable inroads into management.
In the past two decades, re-engineering, business process redesign, and
benchmarking have captured the attention and enthusiasm of mangers,
mainly of middle management, and become globally pervasive.
Unfortunately, because of its call for the radical redesign of work, doing

away with seemingly unnecessary elements, re-engineering became associated with impersonal downsizing. Nevertheless, it represented a major developmental step in systems design.

Reportedly, re-engineering fails 70 percent of the time. That is probably not out of line with most management efforts, and in any case, failures are the inevitable consequence of risk-taking, which itself is highly desirable. But the failures are usually attributed to such factors as operating without higher levels of management being involved in the process, failing to include the views of employees who would be affected, and underestimating the organization's resistance to change. That is, the system design failed to deal with its larger context. Putting it another way, top management failed to provide the necessary environment to support such efforts.

Senior management seldom sees the importance of creating a larger context that is physically and attitudinally congruent with the intent of the system designs, one that would be conducive to the system design's success. In that respect, such technical systems designs are comparable to information technology in the sense that both have been poorly understood and seldom adopted for their own use by top management. Information technology got its start at the bottom of the organization, serving clerical and engineering needs, and has grown like a monster with almost no leadership from the top. While there are exceptions, a great many top executives are still not interested or involved.

Most executives at the top similarly ignore systems design and its offspring. As a result, neither information technology nor systems design has reached its potential. Seldom has either been employed to advance the strategic interests of the organization's top leaders. But if senior executives begin to embrace the mentality that is characteristic of senior designers, they will recognize the importance of seeing these developments in context and will be able to create the larger forms and the appropriate attitudes necessary to sustain them.

The differences between applying a new systems technology such as re-engineering and developing a true design perspective are subtle but important. While technology is involved in almost any design, the crucial and defining aspect of design is its distinction from technology. In the area of human affairs, technique is usually insufficient, if not counterproductive. If professionals come to rely only on technique, they fail. Design, on the other hand, is an approach, a posture. It uses tools sometimes, but most important, it brings a different perspective to a situation, one that studies and embraces the larger environment and gives it new form.

As we have seen, the design of organizations, of societies actually, always follows the available communications technology. When we had to be within earshot of each other, we organized into tribes. Later, with messengers on horseback, the feudal system emerged. Eventually, the postal service was developed, permitting us to have bureaucracy. The advent of telephone and telegraph brought about the international organization. Along the way, other communication advances such as the printing press, typewriters, carbon paper, and xerography all helped shape the design of organizations.

Now the Internet and accompanying information technology present a completely new way to design our organizations. We are enabled, for the first time, to network nongeographically into small groups or into larger overlapping networks of any size. We can make new arrangements and alter old ones by pressing a button. Contrary to popular conceptions, communication among people on this medium can be deeply personal and highly creative. Opportunities abound for management to build on this radically new base, inventing wired and wireless organizations unlike any we have ever experienced.

The implications for social change are profound. This revolutionary technology gives us an entirely new social form in which many of us, perhaps all of us, will live. Achievements in telephonic communication and in broadcasting, as influential as they have been, have not changed our basic social structures. We still live and work in essentially the same configurations we have for a century or more. Computer-based conferencing, however, makes real the long dreamed of ability to function in global communities.

Although hundreds of millions of people now communicate on the Internet, it is much too early to tell just how this development will affect management practices. But it is already clear that work groups collaborating on the Internet become somewhat autonomous and independent, requiring a more tolerant and flexible management style.

One manager, eager to improve the innovative quality of a project team under his supervision, recognized that potentially important contributions were not being elicited from some of the junior or introverted or otherwise marginal members of the team. He decided to forego most of the regular, face-to-face meetings and instead connected project members via computer conferencing technology. He realized that the traditional meetings were forcing these quieter members to sandwich their comments in between the comments of more senior or voluble members, and in those circumstances they were reluctant to come forward. But communicating online, at times convenient to them in an asynchronous manner, gave them freedom from that constraint. As a result, there was not only an increase in participation but in the level and quality of innovation as well.

22
The Hidden
Dynamics of Design

Architects usually carry the thought that when they are designing buildings, they are actually designing organizations. They are right in that. They design experiences, not just rooms; situations, not just spaces; relationships, not just furniture; communities, not just real estate developments. Increasingly, they have come to embrace the concept of social design as central to their work. As Winston Churchill said, "We shape our buildings, and afterwards our buildings shape us."

In organization design, the boundary between physical and social design is disappearing. This means that designers not only have to become leaders and managers, but they must learn to work with representatives from the social sciences and other fields as well, such as philosophy and history. Designers need to acquire not the skills but the perspectives of these professionals.

The top people in any field always transcend technique. A particular outlook energizes their work, a viewpoint toward the challenges they face. For designers it's studying the larger environment and experimenting, modeling, and inventing appropriate forms to meet a particular situation while at the same time honoring the needs and goals of the people involved. So it will increasingly make sense for designers to reach out to other disciplines, some in the humanities, to achieve that fresh outlook that moves them beyond technique.

Some designs are endlessly effective. Meetings held at round tables, for example, will never lose their power to distribute participation more evenly. But other design interventions may depend for their power only upon the fact that they stand in sharp contrast to conventional procedures.

We often forget that almost everything derives its power from its context. A teacher may seem excellent because so many are mediocre. Honesty is so powerful because it exists against a backdrop of almost constant deception. Similarly, a design may work well only as long as it is different from the conventionality of what existed before. But if it becomes the standard way of functioning, it may lose its power. That is why most new management techniques and most new designs, seemingly no matter what they are as long as they are well intended, work for a while and then don't work. And why constant innovation is the continuing requirement of leadership.

Like leadership, design is dynamic, not static. One cannot design a situation and expect it to work indefinitely. Any design requires constant attention and revision, even a seemingly permanent design, such as a house. Seventy percent of new houses are remodeled within three years. Designs involving human relationships are even more in need of continuing modification and improvement.

As illustration of the true nature of management, organization theorist Charles Hampden-Turner points to the scene in *Alice's Adventures in Wonderland* in which the frustrated characters try to play croquet using live flamingos as mallets and hedgehogs as balls. The flamingos and hedgehogs keep moving. Such is the case with social design. The designs involve living beings, and they keep moving.

Better designers always involve the eventual participants in the design process. There are strong practical and ethical reasons for that. On the practical side, not only do these participants know much that would improve the design, but their involvement makes them more likely to make the plan work. They become invested in its success.

The ethical reasons are subtler. For example, when managers know how some act or technique or design they are using is likely to affect employees but the employees don't, managers' respect for those employees predictably erodes. Knowing that employees are being fooled, these managers are blinded to their staff's genuinely intelligent behavior and creativity. Such deception, therefore, fails in two ways. It harms the deceived, but even more pernicious, it harms the deceiver through the gradual erosion of respect for others, even for people in general. Therefore, one solid rule for leaders and managers, and for all who apply social designs, is to operate always so that one's liking and respect for employees can grow. That may be the best case for openness in management and design.

One further caveat: Designs can have unintended consequences, even when they work well. Consider the design decision to establish casual Fridays at work, when dress codes were relaxed. Although the change was quickly embraced, the executives who made such changes were surprised to find that instead of gratitude from employees, they were deluged with new complaints and demands. Why not casual every day? If we can make this change, why not some others long overdue? The change produced rising expectations, as almost every positive management action does. Leaders, like athletes or soldiers, cannot relax after success but must be always ready for a quick turn of events, for the unintended consequences and inevitable paradoxes of leadership.

But isn't a manager's relationship to individual employees crucial to good leadership? Yes, nothing is more important. Won't focusing on social design detract from that emphasis? No, it might facilitate it. Being fully engaged with the people one manages is the essence of good management. Paradoxically, that kind of dedicated engagement is made more possible, indeed more likely, as one dispenses with the ineffective and time-consuming management approaches of the 20th century and instead takes on the role of social architect. The manager who can embrace paradox (remember, in human affairs, paradox is the rule, not the exception) realizes that it is entirely possible to go both directions simultaneously—intensively engaging individuals and, at the same time, designing the larger framework for progress.

Management designs also need to go in opposite directions at once. Just as an architect designing a major building makes sure there are both public and private spaces, managers wanting to redesign their situations need to incorporate the traditional with the new, the familiar with the unfamiliar. When advertising legend Jay Chiat made the radical changes in his agency that eliminated private offices, put everyone on cell phones, and made all spaces public, he famously communicated to both employees and clients that the agency was geared for the new world of constant technological change. In that respect, the design was extremely effective. The design had to be revised, however, because employees found the new arrangements intolerable. They couldn't adjust to having no privacy. Chiat had only moved in one direction.

23

Beware of Experts

A s you will be increasingly called to apply your design talents to areas in which you have not before worked, such as in improving social infrastructure, and therefore need to inform yourself about psychology, sociology, anthropology, economics, political science, and many other subjects that pertain, you will obviously need to consult experts. But I would like to suggest that you exercise caution in your choice and in the way in which you use what you learn.

The truth about expertise is highly disturbing. Experts in all fields, even in design, are not just often wrong, we are usually wrong. Sometimes almost all of us are wrong. As science and knowledge progress, our strongly held positions are regularly overturned. But we are slow to catch up. Few of us understand the latest research in any detail. The average scientific journal article is read by only seven people. That means most of us acquire our understanding of a new study from conversations or from media reports, which never reveal the full complexities or qualifications of the findings.

This lag in learning is a serious failing. At the Massachusetts Institute of Technology, they say that half of what freshmen learn is obsolete by the time they get to be juniors. It is probably not far off the mark to suggest that any experts still doing what they were trained to do are well behind where they need to be. And the continuing education requirements now mandated by most professions, creating a stream of business income for those running the programs, have been shown to have no positive effect on design practice, so probably have no positive effect on other professions either.

The saddest part of the picture is that even when experts are aware of the research, public pressure of one form or another often forces them to take actions they know are wrong. Sometimes the pressure is political. Educators regularly compromise their better judgment, ignoring research that would require change; they continue giving grades, assigning homework, paddling disobedient students, teaching creationism instead of evolution, and so forth because parents and school board members and politicians controlling the funds insist. By the same token, correctional officers continue to enforce the death penalty even though they know it is ineffective in deterring crime; they do so because the public believes the political demagogues who continue to mislead in this regard.

Sometimes the pressure comes from the market, where profit seems most likely to be made. As we have seen in our discussion of commoditization, most professions have moved closer to a business model, sometimes losing their professional way in the process. Because of the way the market operates, urban planners continue to accept designs for the creation of giant shopping centers, discount houses, and retail superstores they know will destroy existing communities and for sprawling land developments they know will never become true communities. Physicians are now controlled by corporate HMOs and make their money not by listening, thinking, and advising but only by doing medical procedures, very often the wrong ones. Psychotherapists have to supply phony diagnoses to be paid by health insurance. Lawyers seeking larger incomes have made us the most litigious society on earth. Members of all professions are increasingly willing to abandon their professional judgment to accommodate what the public is willing to pay for.

Finally, we cannot ignore the fact that experts, even the best ones, simply disagree ... not just sometimes but often. And their disagreements are usually not trivial but fundamental. They often take directly opposing views even after examining the research evidence and on issues that matter greatly, including ethnic differences, capital punishment, economic planning, child rearing, political systems, medical treatment, organizational leadership, educational strategies, religious practices, and urban design, to say nothing of major ideological differences that dominate many expressions of expertise.

Here is a paradox. It would seem that the less we know as professionals, the more willing we are to give firm advice. For example, the top people in the physical sciences, who have a base of solid knowledge, are more circumspect when it comes to giving advice than are, for example, human relations experts, whose knowledge is less solid, more controversial. TV talk shows showcase such human relations advisors by the dozens, and I can tell you that being in that field, I find most of what I watch to be completely unfounded in solid knowledge.

One of my mentors and colleagues, social psychologist Alex Bavelas, commented to me once about the fact that if physicists are asked about a problem, they will generally say that they could study it, that it might take a couple of years and that they might be able to offer some good probabilities at the end of that time. But, Bavelas continued, when psychologists are asked about a human relations problem (which is usually more complex and difficult than physics), they will either try to provide an answer right then and there, shooting from the hip as it were, or indicate they would need only a few weeks to study it and give a firm conclusion. The paradox is that the less one knows, the more likely one will offer expert advice quickly and with confidence. Being tentative reflects strength, not weakness.

In considering expertise, we should not ignore the fact that it is notoriously difficult to predict anything, especially the future, as Yogi Berra would say. Some would say it's impossible. Writer and filmmaker Michael Crichton makes that case when considering the difficulties of 100-year projections of any kind. As part of his questioning of expertise, he simply lists a number of terms that people 100 years ago had never heard of: airport, antibiotic, antenna, computer, continental drift, tectonic plates, zipper, radio, television, robot, video, virus, gene, proton, neutron, atomic structure, quark, atomic bomb, nuclear energy, ecosystem, jumpsuits, fingerprints, jet stream, shell shock, shock wave, microwave, tidal wave, IUD, DVD, MP3, MRI, HIV, SUV, VHS, heart transplant, liposuction, laser, penicillin, Internet, nylon, lap dancing, gene therapy, bipolar, moonwalk, Prozac, sunscreen, fiber optic, direct dialing, urban legends. Given that change is accelerating, foreseeing the next 100 years would be even more presumptuous.

Add to all this the fact that experts, like all specialists, are distributed on a normal curve, with abilities ranging from excellent to poor, from genius to dangerous. So while dealing with experts can be most illuminating, it can also be like walking through a mine field.

Designers as Social
Psychologists

C ompared to the lawful, predictable behavior of things in the physical world, the behavior of human beings in the social world often appears irrational, unpredictable, confusing. And indeed it is. Completely different assumptions than those used for the physical world are required to approach an understanding of human behavior. Often these assumptions are counterintuitive, not conforming at all to popular ideas.

Let's suppose a team becomes involved in the design of a new communication system. It would be helpful for them to consider some of the understandings that come from social psychology in terms of what we know about communication among humans.

What follows, then, is an attempt to make clear the assumptions that might guide such a team of designers, assumptions that will help make the behavior understandable even if it is seemingly irrational at the outset. It is essential for methodological reasons that we spell out these guiding principles as carefully as we can so that we enter the communication design process with a checklist of reminders about the counterintuitive aspects of human affairs. That should keep us from making more mistakes than we need to.

Human behavior is paradoxical. This bears repeating because it is a major theme of metadesign, and we have referred to it repeatedly already. But let's just take one example from communication to remind us of its paradoxical nature. For instance, only a good communicator would say something like, "We just can't communicate." People who really can't communicate don't know they can't.

Nothing is as invisible as the obvious. The most important discoveries come from taking a fresh look at what most people take for granted. One reason the prediction of human affairs is so difficult is because future trends tend to be based on present conditions. But present conditions are largely invisible even to those who spend their lives looking at them. In 1967, two of the most respected futurists, Herman Kahn and Anthony Wiener, published a book titled *The Year* 2000. In it there is no mention whatever of energy, pollution, environment, ecology, women's rights—all issues that were to become highly visible the very next year, let alone the year 2000. The fact that we are living in the present does not mean we know what that present is. For that matter, the fact that we are something (man, woman, black, child, etc.) doesn't mean we know what that something is. We need in each instance to have our consciousness raised before we can even know who or what we are. We all live in a communication environment, but because it is so obvious to us, it becomes invisible. The first task always is to make the invisible visible and that means trying to see what is so obvious it is invisible.

Human affairs succumb to fashion. In analyzing trends, it is irresistibly tempting to extrapolate on a linear basis, assuming current growth will continue in a straight line indefinitely. Human behavior, however, moves in cycles or phases, often returning to its original state or lower. This is most clearly seen in the fashion of clothing design, in which trends repeat on a periodic basis. But as writer Tom Wolfe has often pointed out, all is fashion. All human events, even such fundamental ones as politics and family life, are subject to fashion. Indeed, communication is itself vulnerable to fashion—both in structure (who says what to whom) and in content (what kinds of things are said). For example, families today discuss matters that would never have been permissible a few generations ago. Because of breakthroughs of the labor movement, the same is true for business organizations.

Technology backfires. Although we live in a climate of technological optimism, believing in our capacity to create a technological fix for all our problems, the fact is that even when technology succeeds, it usually backfires in some way, often worsening the very situation it was introduced to correct. Widening highways to reduce congestion, for example, increases the congestion not only on the highways but in the villages they connect. Air conditioning pollutes the air as well as conditions it. Hospitals and physicians create illness as well as cure it. Communication technology is not exempt from this phenomenon. Opening areas of personal communication can enhance relationships but also damage them. Experiencing communication breakthroughs can escalate expectations about future communication that are unattainable, producing the kind of discontent that ruptures relationships, often terminating them.

Messages always carry metamessages. As we have noted, metamessages sent by the form of communication can be more powerful than the original intent of the content of the message. Hidden messages, often unintended, therefore exist in every communication, sometimes producing negative results. Communication programs that educate people about marriage, child rearing, or sex can so increase one's sense of responsibility in an area where one is largely helpless that it predictably leads to abuse. We pointed earlier to parent training as an example of how skill training can make parents treat their children more harshly. This is not because the content of the program told them to but due to the frustration they feel as a result of the metamessage from the instructor, that parenthood is doable. *I know how to do it and you can learn it, too* is the message even if the instructor never uses those words. The metamessage is sent by the simple fact that the course exists and the instructor is there. Parents' new sense of responsibility may contrast so sharply with what they actually seem to be able to do that the ensuing feelings of frustration lead them to take actions that are abusive. It is incumbent on us, therefore, to be mindful not only of the regular communication but of the concomitant metacommunication, which is likely to be even more determining of learning in the long run.

The meaning and power of communication are derived from its context. All meaning, of course, is dependent on context, on figure/ground relationships. Something stands out because of the background against which we see it. The same is true for communication. If there has been a general absence of communication among a particular group of people, almost any communication will seem important and rich. It stands out as figure against ground. That is why episodes of honest communication between people can be so powerful—they exist in the context of dishonesty, of deception, tact, and small talk. This then becomes a vital design consideration. If a communication seems valuable because it is uncommon, then making it common turns figure into ground and may therefore defeat the design intention. Occasional messages from the president of the organization may be very powerful, but if they are made frequently, they it may lose their power.

Optimize, not maximize. Although the human tendency in planning is to maximize what seems beneficial, it is probably wiser in most circumstances to optimize. Successful human relations tend to operate on curvilinear, not linear, projections—optimizing, not maximizing. In human communication one can get too much of a good thing. Organizational communication is a good example of this. We have long operated on the assumption that when it comes to open communication, the more, the better. The evidence does not support this assumption, however. It is clear that when all lines of communication are open, confusion reigns. In fact, a little bit of certain kinds of communication can go a very long way. So the design mandate is to optimize the amount of communication depending on type and based on what participants find helpful.

With increased experience comes the need for control. The development of the automatic transmission was a major achievement in automotive history. Yet people who are the most experienced drivers, who drive for pleasure or for a vocation, eschew the automatic and want instead a manual transmission, "four-on-the-floor," even if it costs more. That is, they want the control themselves; they want to feel that they are driving the car. We find much the same phenomenon with users' reactions to microcomputer communication software that automates complicated functions, often to one keystroke. Mature users usually prefer to drive it themselves and like the idea of exploring the complexities of the system manually. It is important, therefore, for us to remember that not all people will necessarily accept the easy way. Automating communication functions is appropriate for amateur and beginner users and for certain functions but may not be appropriate for mature users. As with other fields in communication, the easy way may not be the better way. It's worth noting the opposite phenomenon in leadership and management. The more experienced and senior the executives, the less they concern themselves with interpersonal control, and the more interested they are in the larger issues of goals and institutional health.

Conserving human resources is a design priority. As we approach the design of communication systems for organizations, we first identify the most important human resources of the organization (usually the leaders and more creative members) and make as certain as possible that these vital resources are protected. This is necessary because it is remarkably easy to use up those resources inadvertently through the misapplication of communication. For example, British anthropologist Mary Douglas pointed out important differences between participative and hierarchical organizations in the way decisions are made, risks are assessed, people are treated. She would hold, for example, that participative communication systems tend to bring attacks on the stronger members, often on the leaders, while more hierarchical systems bring attacks on the weaker members. Neither hierarchical nor participatory systems are "better" in any permanent, fundamental sense, but each must be used appropriately to the situation, to meet particular goals, and with the conservation of human resources in mind. When I ask a group to identify its most important resources, the members almost always mention the leader and the most creative colleagues. So it matters a great deal how the communication system fosters or prevents the abuse of those resources. Reminded of this, the group tends to find ways to protect them.

Systems must be more user-determined. Most computer systems, even those involving human communication, have been designed for users, but not by users. Seldom is the user even consulted in the design process. The typical system has been designed by "experts" using a rational analysis of both the problem and the technical capability of the system components. But the user represents an important voice. Time and again we rediscover the basic psychological principle (however counterintuitive it may be) that the greatest resource for the solution of any problem is the very population that has the problem.

Problems vs. predicaments in human affairs. Design is often equated with the solution of problems. But in human affairs, as philosopher Abraham Kaplan indicated, most troubles are not problems but predicaments—permanent, inescapable, paradoxical dilemmas. Predicaments don't yield to problem-solving approaches characterized by analysis and technical applications. Different approaches are required. Indeed, treating predicaments as if they were problems can make matters worse. Predicaments arise not by something going wrong but by something going right. Crime, for example, is not a problem but a predicament. It comes not so much from the pathologies of society as it does from the successes of society—from increased individual freedom, affluence, mobility, urbanization, communication, and so on. Those aspects of society that we tend to value most. Predicaments also are marked by the fact that they are made worse by society's efforts to handle them. Again, crime is a good example. Our efforts to combat crime actually increase it: Prisons harden criminals, most of whom return to prison after being released and committing a more serious crime, and unless police walk the beat and become friendly with members of the community, their presence can actually increase criminal behavior. As we approach the design of communication systems to enable people to reach higher planes of living, to overcome traditional barriers to personal and organizational effectiveness, it will serve us well to be reminded that we may be dealing with predicaments, not problems.

Communication always interacts with a larger system. Communication cannot be seen as separate from the larger context in which it is imbedded. Communication influences and is influenced by political, social, cultural, and economic conditions and must be viewed in terms of these interdependencies. Therefore, a systems approach to design of communication is necessary. This means, first of all, that communication cannot be considered neutral but always acts either to sustain or alter (deepen, reinforce, weaken, modify) existing systems. For example, opening lines of communication that encourage free expression of feeling in a relationship in which the power of communicators is unequal is likely to lead to increased vulnerability of the less powerful and consequently increased power of the already powerful. It is necessary therefore to study the possible system implications and to adopt a position relative to the desired social outcomes of any communication design.

People want more of what they already have. Although the participant in the communication process is certainly in the best position to assess his or her own needs, certain tendencies toward error systematically enter the human equation. One of these is the tendency to choose not what one needs but what one already has, often in great abundance. People want more of what are already their long suits. Beautiful people want to be more attractive, articulate people want more fluency, learned people want more education, and rich people want more money. This phenomenon may be particularly true in the area of communication. People seem to want what they already have even if they don't think so. In developing methods of inquiry to identify desired communication capabilities, therefore, we must be aware of this possible source of both insight and error. Related to this is the phenomenon that people need to transform the strange into the familiar, which we have discussed earlier, even when they don't like the familiar—such as structured committee meetings. This is important for the design of communication systems because people may steer away from the options that new technology may afford them by clinging to old social forms.

People need "inaccurate" communication. Central to the maintenance of any relationship or institution is the need for communication that may deceive or distort. Such communication may be just as important, perhaps even more important, than accurate information transfer because the culture of an organization is sustained by fiction as well as fact. Just as social interactions are lubricated by tactfulness and white lies, organizations are maintained and enhanced by myth and mystique. It is fundamentally necessary for people to believe things about themselves and each other that are untrue. Romance, for example, requires mystique—it requires not knowing some things and believing other things that are not true about oneself and one's partner. Deception, including self-deception, while it may be dysfunctional or pathological at times, is often highly functional, vital to the health of organizations at all levels. Similarly, there is an important role for selective communication, distortion, and secrecy in organizational life. Information systems designed without these considerations in mind could, for example, bypass middle management and supply the top and the bottom of the organization with complete and accurate information about each other. But middle management is the carrier of the culture of the organization, playing a complex role in filtering, buffering, and massaging the information so that the top of the organization can continue to maintain useful fictions about what is going on at the bottom and vice versa. Without a mechanism to introduce these creative human inventions, organizations could not survive. The primary function of communication is to build and sustain community, but accurate information systems are not always an ally in this effort.

It is likely that accurate information transfer (veridicality between what is sent and what is received) actually plays only a small part in the overall functioning of communication systems. Information often becomes radically distorted in the communication process, and it often does so on a systematic basis. Needs of all types, not the least of which are psychological, shape the perception of information. Beyond the simple (or complex) distortions to fit particular personal or organizational needs, communication can also perform other functions, sometimes even when the communication is not understood or even received. The appearance of our name on a routing slip, for example, can serve to bolster our ego and reassure us that we are still in the communication hierarchy. Communication is used for covering up as well as exposing. If any executive were to direct an employee, "Tell me three things I don't want to hear," the employee would probably have little difficulty obliging. It may be as important to block communication as it is to transmit it.

Communication is both verbal and paraverbal. We all know that glance and gesture—body language—can add substantially to the meaning of communication in a face-to-face setting. What is less well known is that in the absence of such opportunities for sending visual cues we unconsciously take pains to supply the same subtlety and nuance to voice-only communication (such as telephone calls) by speech inflections, pauses, laughs, and the like—what is called "paraverbal" communication. When communication lacks both visual and auditory cues, such as computer-mediated text communication, people continue to introduce paraverbal communication to ensure meaning by sometimes adding parenthetical comments, such as <grin> and all manner of icons to communicate mood and meaning and to make sure the recipient does not mistake the intended joke for an insult. The design of future electronic communication systems should take into account this natural compensatory activity and provide for it. Then perhaps we will find ways to joke online that are simply too risky at the present state of the technology.

Given the choice between accessing data or other individuals, people will choose each other. A common misconception of the information needs of members of organizations, particularly of senior executives, holds that people want access to databases, to libraries of information at their fingertips. Time and again, however, when they have the choice between databases and people, they more often choose people. The higher one goes in an organization, the more one relies on the opinions, interpretations, and advice of one's trusted colleagues. Failure to recognize this fact, believing that executives want information rather than communication, has led to the development of management information systems that ignore completely the strategic issues of the organization because executives responsible for those strategic decisions do not participate in the information system. It does not give them what they want, which is each other. Computerized information providers designed to provide easy access to a variety of databases and only incidentally make it possible for network members to communicate with each other find that 60 percent of the activity is people talking to each other. This is true even when few or no measures are taken to stimulate or aid such communication. People simply choose each other over databases. Whatever systems are invented must take into account that people will consistently choose communication over information. MySpace and YouTube are good examples of the importance of this motivation.

The more something matters, the less programmable it becomes. Once again, in human terms, the more significant a relationship is, the less skill plays a part in it. Our most important human affairs—marriage, child rearing, education, leadership—defy our attempts to technologize them. Technology may be sufficient for lower-order human events—training, advertising—but not for those we value most. Those events require the transcendence of technique, often its very opposite—loss of control, lack of information, and an increase in personal vulnerability. Technique is required for seduction but is useless in true romance. So for the less significant aspects of human affairs, data and information play an important role. For the more significant affairs, however, knowledge and wisdom are required. It may be, therefore, that we will find ourselves less able to program communication arrangements for the most valued and desired of human experiences in terms of both physical and social technology.

Individuals are strong, organizations are fragile. We've seen earlier that it's almost impossible to damage an individual permanently, but it takes very little to destroy a relationship or an organization. The implication, therefore, is that we must take special care to guard against the possibility that messages might become missiles, creating wreckage of the delicate network of relationships that make up any organization.

Evaluate the success of communication systems on the quality of discontent engendered. Work in human affairs is often frustrating because we expect our successes to produce satisfaction on the part of those we try to help, but it seldom does (not for long, anyway). The paradox we must recognize is that improvement in human affairs leads not to satisfaction but to discontent, albeit a higher-order discontent than might have existed before. The history of revolutions, for example, shows that they happen not when conditions are at their lowest ebb but only after things have gotten better, reforms have been instituted, leadership developed, and the populace has come to have a new vision of what might be. It is what historians have labeled the theory of rising expectations, and it fuels the fires of revolution and change because it creates a discrepancy between what one has and what one now has come to see it is possible to have. That discrepancy is the source of discontent and the motor for change. Psychotherapy works the same way. Successful therapy leads not to satisfaction but to higher-order discontent. That is, as one solves the lower-order problem and concerns, one becomes discontented about higher issues, issues having to do with self-actualization. So in organizations, for example, if management has instituted improvements, we may find the discontent moving from concern about working conditions (*It is too hot in here* or *I don't get paid enough*) to what psychologist Abraham Maslow called "meta-grumbles," concerns about needs for self-actualization (*I don't feel that I'm in on things enough here* or *I don't think my talents are being fully utilized*). Only in an organization in which people are in on things and their talents are being utilized does it occur to someone to complain about those issues. Therefore, we must, in these paradoxical human affairs, learn to evaluate our achievements not on the satisfaction and gratitude they produce but on our ability to produce movement from lower-order discontent to higher-order discontent.

Managing Innovation and its Partner, Failure

As designers expand their horizons and enter new fields very different from the ones with which they have become familiar, they will need to take many risks they haven't had to take before. That is a threatening idea because designs are not supposed to fail. Indeed, as designers have submitted to corporate ways of doing business, they are usually legally liable for any failures. But taking risks is necessary at all stages of the design and building process and always has been. And risk-taking always involves some failure. The buildings of leading architects have often leaked badly, and the cost of repairing legendary architect Frank Lloyd Wright's most famous design, Falling Water, has run into the millions. Architecture icon Frank Gehry was sued by MIT for failings of his $350 million Stata Center, which received considerable critical praise.

Where did we get the idea that design shouldn't fail? Other professions fail all the time but are not necessarily punished. If any profession shouldn't fail, surely it would be healthcare. Countless times the treatment strategies do not work, but there is no penalty. Even medical mistakes are seldom questioned. Yet as we discussed, 2 million medical mistakes annually account for one-fifth of all hospital admissions and include at least 100,000 deaths. These are in addition to the casualties of physician-induced illness such as side effects of drugs, complications from surgery, and catching a staph infection while in the hospital.

Compared to medicine, design is as safe as being in your mother's arms.

The important reason we must take a different posture toward failure is this: *Failure is necessary for innovation.* Innovation always requires risk-taking, and risk always involves failure. The great innovators failed many times before succeeding.

We can learn much from Charles Kettering, a leading American inventor—responsible for the automotive self-starter, refrigerants, diesel engines, home air conditioners—with some 150 or more patents to his credit. He thought that genuine innovators were hobbled more than helped by what they learned in school and that students subjected to the prospect of failing exams and "flunking out" learned a bad lesson: Failure is terminal. A good research man, he would say, failed every time but the last one. If he failed 999 times before finally succeeding, it was only the last one that mattered.

The most successful entrepreneurs have failed at least once. One of them, David Levy, said that when he was working for Apple Computers, his boss told him he wasn't failing enough, and that from now on he wanted to see an 80 percent failure rate. Thomas Watson Sr., founder of IBM, said, "The fastest way to success is to double your failure rate." Author and filmmaker Michael Crichton says, "If you don't fail a certain percentage of the time, it means you're playing it too safe." Athletes know this. If tennis players don't serve some double faults or if skiers never fall, it means they are not taking the necessary risks to perform at their very best.

The legendary Purdue University basketball coach Piggy Lambert once told his player John Wooden, who eventually became a legendary coach himself, "Remember, the team that makes the most mistakes is probably going to win." He meant that they were going to try harder, risk tactics and strategies, take more shots. Wooden never forgot that lesson, and he employed it with his 10 national championship teams at UCLA.

If we are to bring about change, we will certainly have to become less averse to risk and more tolerant of failure. Design firms have been going through a series of management fads beginning with quality circles and total quality management and then on to zero defects and Six

Sigma, all driving toward performance close to perfection. But innovation involves trial and error, and it is riddled with mistakes and wrong turns. How those experiences are handled by management determines just how innovative the organization can become.

Corporate giant 3M attributes much of its success to its acceptance, even encouragement, of failure. Its most famous example is Post-it Notes, which were the product of a failed adhesive, too weak for the work intended but later seen as perfect for the concept of semi-adhesive paper. Think of the cultural change that could happen in design if the 3M attitudes of encouraging failure were adopted. It may be difficult to imagine a design school or design firm embracing that attitude, a professor or manager taking a genuine, nonjudgmental interest in a well-intended effort that failed. But that attitude is strong in the history of innovation and is spreading in business and industry. We can take a lesson from the Wright brothers. They were as excited about their failures as they were about their successes.

Management theorist Warren Bennis interviewed dozens of CEOs to determine what made them successful, and he found that their attitude toward failure was often a key. He quotes one of them as saying, "If I have an art form of leadership, it is to make as many mistakes as quickly as I can in order to learn."

Making the necessary changes in design education and practice will require a special courage, the courage to alter a program that seems to be working for something that might work better. As social theorist Marshall McLuhan famously said, "If it's working, it's obsolete." So the saying, "If it ain't broke, don't fix it" must become "If it ain't broke, fix it anyway."

There may be a way out of the liability problem. Architect and attorney Jerry Weisbach tells me that he has in the past been able to modify contract language (for a very innovative architect) in such a way as to change the burden of care to allow for innovation. He says, "The problem with the present standard of care is that all it takes is another professional to testify that the 'ordinary' standard of care was not met. Such testimony is readily available on the open 'expert' market."

"Years ago," he says, "I reviewed a U.S. government contract which provided that if informed by the architect or engineer that the design included an innovative idea or technology and the government agreed to the inclusion of that idea or technology, then the standard of care governing the service would change from negligence to gross negligence. Since it would be very difficult to prove gross negligence, it allowed the design professional great protection from liability suits. The fear, and it is real, of professional negligence suits is an important and effective detriment to innovation."

Conflict Resolution or Conflict Management?

C onflicts come in many forms, but for our purposes here I would like to distinguish between two main types: Type I, which arise out of an immediate difficulty that is time bound and in which the goals may be the same between the two conflicting groups, and Type II, which arise out of longstanding opposition and in which the goals of the two groups may be importantly different.

Two examples of the first type: failing to explain the reasons behind a management act, which led to misunderstandings that could be cleared up through improved communication, and hiring a manager who violates expectations to such a degree that his removal seems necessary to resolve the conflict. In short, these are conflicts that have a root cause that can fairly easily be discovered and dealt with through better communication and problem-solving approaches.

Type II conflict, which can grow out of sometimes centuries-old animosities and be so complex as to defy analysis, are exemplified by ethnic battles such as those in the Middle East and Fiji or by the disputes between management and labor. In these cases, the situation cannot be cleared up simply through more accurate communication because at least some of the goals of the two parties are not shared, and the injuries through the years have been so painful that to rehearse them exacerbates the difficulties.

Our distinction between problems and predicaments is relevant here. You will recall that problems have an identifiable root cause, like a diseased process, and can be treated and solved. Predicaments, on the other hand, are permanent, inescapable, paradoxical dilemmas. Sometimes they arise out of factors that are not troubles but strengths. Predicaments cannot be solved because they are not problems in the first place. They can only be coped with. So Type I conflicts are problems, Type II are predicaments. We can solve Type I, but we can only cope with Type II.

Rather than refer generally to this area of work as conflict resolution, let's make a distinction between Type I and Type II conflicts. While the term "conflict resolution" might apply to Type I, it does not to Type II, where the most we can expect is to cope more effectively, more humanely, less violently. In other words, with Type II conflict, we offer to manage it rather than promise to resolve it.

Experience in any effort to improve human relations has shown over and over again that quick fixes tend not to last and that the only approaches to change that are uniformly effective are those that involve the parties in a continuing discipline of some sort. For example, brief psychiatric treatment to cure alcoholics works less well than Alcoholics Anonymous, which keeps a continuing discipline at its core. Similarly, crash diets don't work, but disciplined lifelong changes in eating habits do. The practice of bodybuilding, yoga, meditation, coaching are all in that disciplined practice category, while counseling, psychotherapy, and weekend workshops are not. The same is true in conflict management. Efforts to bring about peaceful solutions to Type II conflicts must be augmented with continuing discipline, mechanisms to ensure that the efforts won in the peace agreements can be continually reinforced.

The principals in some conflicts are so burdened by restrictions and expectations imposed by their constituencies that they cannot fully explore their experiences, feelings, desires, and options, nor can they compromise or make agreements without going back to their respective constituencies. But in certain circumstances, such as the conflict between Protestants and Catholics in Northern Ireland, is was possible for documentary filmmaker Bill McGaw to gather representatives (not leaders) of the warring factions together to discuss the issues, which led to his making the television program "The Steel Shutter." In this way, through the use of what we might call a shadow group, he was able to introduce into public awareness the deeper feelings of responsible participants as well as their willingness to hear each others' concerns and reach out for connections that would be difficult for the leaders to exhibit. Such a dramatic exposure of how people feel, what they really want, and what they are willing to accept can alter public discourse and thereby encourage and empower their leaders to make adjustments in line with the new public awareness. Employing such shadow groups can occasionally be a useful approach, especially if the discussion is managed in a way to broadcast it widely to the interested parties.

It is widely believed that leader-led, face-to-face confrontation and communication is required for resolution of conflict. At WBSI however, we have discovered that other media can be equal to or in some instances better than such discourse. We have used quite a few media, but perhaps the most effective of have been our experiments with discussions, educational programs, task forces, and community groups created on the Internet. This medium, often maligned as impersonal and dehumanizing, proved in our hands to be highly personal, intimate, and decidedly constructive of sound and lasting personal relationships. Community groups (similar to therapy groups) started by us online more than two decades ago are still functioning. The Internet gives us a simple, inexpensive way to create online communities nongeographically. And in discussions of subject matter that embody built-in conflicts, such as abortion, we were able to create a task force that was extremely effective, one that in a face-to-face circumstance would certainly have foundered in acrimony and polarization. So through the use of face-to-face meetings augmented with multimedia strategies such as radio, television, telephone, and most especially the Internet, we have the instruments with which to establish the continuing dialogues necessary for conflict management.

Designers may have special difficulty dealing with this concept because they are constantly reminded that their training and professional responsibility is in solving problems, certainly not in attending to predicaments. But metadesign, as it addresses the larger issues in human affairs, will often be confronting predicaments, and we must enlarge the perspective of all design education programs to embrace that new responsibility and that new area of design competence.

Part VI
The Radical Redesign of Design Education

D esign education is always under discussion and dispute. The use of traditional charettes, close-knit studio teams, tough critiques, assignments that can be fulfilled only by many overnight sessions, the lack of representation of certain disciplines (such as social scientists)—all are often challenged. There has been plenty of disagreement, and it continues. Clearly, the honoring of traditions remains an important motivator to many professors. One development is disturbing: In architecture, few who graduate decide to go forward into licensed practice. That could be for many reasons, including the requirement that they must spend years in low-paying internships before they can even call themselves architects. Or it could be that the advanced computer skills architecture students learned now equip them for other kinds of work, such as special effects technicians in motion picture production.

I would enjoy a discussion of the structural or curricular changes that might be desirable to produce the creative, broad-ranging intellects able to address the larger social and political issues that metadesign calls for. It's been suggested that a completely separate curriculum for what we are calling metadesign be formed and accredited, as different from architecture as public health is from medicine. I can imagine and I look forward to many interesting discussions on that subject. But for the purposes of this book, I would like to approach the issue by addressing what I believe to be the feature of all educational programs we find most difficult to get around in any discussion of change. If we can surmount this barrier, we can design almost any kind of curriculum we choose.

To my mind, the major difficulty is posed by the fundamental devotion to evaluation as a necessary and pervasive component of education. If we can transcend that dimension, I suspect we will have a much better chance at producing the kind of creative designers that metadesign requires. Let's take a look at it, beginning by building from the previous chapter on the necessary role of failure.

The Importance of Failure

The problem we face in today's education generally and design education specifically is not too much failure but too little. We need much more failure at all levels—more failing students, failing instructors, failing administrators. We need to fail sooner, faster, bigger.

The need for failure, for risk-taking, for well-intended mistakes, runs deeper than just management concerns. It penetrates the learning process itself and affects every student. Punishing or penalizing failure guarantees that the learning process will never be as experimental, creative, and risky as it needs to be.

The kind of learning we care most about, the kind that leads to literacy, understanding, awareness, discovery, and personal growth—to wisdom, if you will—is inherently threatening. True education always poses that special kind of threat arising from the entirely realistic fear that after this learning experience, one's life will not be the same. It can happen in the earliest years and is a genuine threat, requiring courage and risk. That level of learning is not common in today's education because it can take place only in an atmosphere of acceptance and safety, inspired by a motivated and knowledgeable instructor and pursued with the freedom of self-direction. It will always involve many mistakes and failures. Our current educational designs do not often permit such explorations.

The concepts of success and failure are so much a part of schooling that it is difficult to imagine what education might be like without them, but these terms should be dropped from the lexicon of educators. Their disappearance would affect everything we do as students, professors, and administrators and, I believe, very much for the better. Neither concept serves us well, nor is either experienced in the way most believe they are. Both are the enemies of intellectual development. Because they were introduced to serve purposes having little to do with learning, they do not belong in the repertory of educators' responses. Beginning with the earliest ages, children who after many failed tries experience the thrill of writing their own names for the first time or spelling a long word do not need gold stars. College students, unless they have been so programmed to work only for praise (and these days some have), will also find intrinsic rewards in the personal accomplishment of building a working model or solving a difficult problem to be completely satisfying without the need for outside evaluations.

As you look back over your life you will discover that success and failure are sometimes indistinguishable and highly interdependent. I had an occasion to do just that when I was invited to a college reunion. To prepare for it, everyone in our class was asked to submit a paragraph describing what had happened to us since graduation. I first composed a paragraph touching some of the predictable points—family, homes, jobs, achievements—but when I finished I thought it read too much like a resumé. Why would I write to my old classmates with such self-serving half-truths? So instead (mainly for my own amusement because I knew the college wouldn't use it) I decided to write my experience the way it really happened. What resulted were several pages full of descriptions of failures, leading to successes, leading to failures, continuing right up to the present. I was struck by how necessary the failures were to my development. Often it was difficult to say which was which because what seemed a failure or success at one point became the opposite later. I'm sure that if we were completely honest we would each have such a story to tell.

As basketball star Michael Jordan says, "I've missed more than 9,000 shots in my career. I've lost about 300 games. Twenty-six times I've been trusted to take the game winning shot and missed. I've failed over and over and over again in my life. And that is why I succeed."

The issue, of course, is the pernicious role of evaluation. That is what defines our failures, essentially criminalizing them. It is entrenched in all of education, and with the growth of concern over accountability, it becomes even more prominent and more inhibiting. Ambrose Bierce, writing his *Devil's Dictionary* a century ago, defined accountability as "the mother of caution."

Evaluation has come to dominate school programs both formally and informally, its putative importance taken for granted by students, educators, and the public. Every aspect of student activity is evaluated, and much of it is graded and reported. Any question answered by a student is typically met with some evaluative comment such as "Good" or "Right." In K-12, even classroom behavior is graded, and in college it is certainly evaluated. In short, every move a student makes academically or socially is subject to evaluation.

Many, perhaps most, of the reasons for evaluation are not pedagogical but stem from the management requirements of the educational system and even more from the larger system in which it is embedded. Employers and graduate schools want to know the letter grades of applying students' performance. But some of it comes from the belief that there exist certain basic skills and information that students must acquire, and it is for the benefit of the student as well as for the larger system requirements that this acquisition be verified by evaluation.

This belief is founded on the premise we have questioned before, that all students should become alike in certain ways, learning the same skills and information to meet established standards. As long as we view education in this way it makes perfect sense for us to measure student progress toward that goal. Evaluation helps the teacher diagnose students' needs and provide feedback to them.

But we make no distinction between basic skills and other kinds of learning—all is subject to evaluation and grading. Our ability to measure achievement in learning basic skills has led to our extending that idea of measurement to the full range of learning. Our evaluative posture toward learning about Shakespeare or the work of a design icon is essentially the same as learning to add a column of numbers or an engineering formula.

We pay a terrible but largely invisible price for indulging in that measurement approach to education. Think about it. Ultimately, do we want graduates to be alike? No. We want them to be different from each other. That's what real education is all about.

Education is the marriage of a person's experience to important concepts. That marriage, that special integration of ideas with experience, forms a unique individual unlike anyone else. Students bring to the learning situation a large mass of previously assimilated experience and understanding that shapes whatever they see and do and therefore whatever they learn. In educating them, we do not want them to be like everyone else but to become whatever their own potential might afford them. We want to individualize them as much as possible. It is in our interest as a society for them to become different from everyone else. It certainly fits our interest in developing creative designers.

While teaching basic skills (what we usually call training) is directed toward making people alike, true education makes them different. Standardized testing, therefore, can apply only to training. We cannot assess individual development by applying standards to students we want to be different from each other. But where do we draw the line? At what point does training become education? Instructors are faced with a dilemma. How can they tell when to shift from the evaluative posture that seems efficacious when teaching skills to the non-evaluative posture required for education, at which point evaluation clearly becomes the enemy of learning? And what system would permit such a shift?

I'm afraid we may not be able to draw that line, and if we seriously think about it, we may decide it is unwise to treat any learning situation evaluatively, even basic skills. Though we would be tempted to employ such measurement to assess performance in basic skills, we may not be seeing skill development in all of its potential richness. In evaluating it, we might be limiting the independent growth of students just as we are doing in what seem to be the more advanced areas of learning, such as literature, social studies, history, and design aesthetics. Maybe we do not want everyone to develop skills in the same way.

No Pure Skills

C learly, there are skills that can be learned, perhaps must be learned, and we can test to see if students do indeed learn them. But paradoxically, that statement, like most significant statements, is both true and false, and it may not be true at the most important levels of learning. It may be that in every situation that involves skill there is also an educational component adding the kind of complexity that makes people different from each other, therefore beyond the realm of standards and evaluation.

Let's take a few examples. I first thought that learning a language was clearly a testable skill. Presumably, we want students to learn how to pronounce the words exactly the way native speakers do. Sophisticated and experienced language teachers, however, do not just teach the language as a skill, they also teach the culture in which the language is embedded. The reason is that without understanding the subtleties and nuances of culture, we cannot understand the true meaning of the communication. Unless we understand that the word *mañana* (formal definition: tomorrow morning) used by a native Spanish speaker may not mean tomorrow morning but something more like "someday soon" or "later" or "eventually" or maybe "never," we could be greatly misled. Similarly, negotiating with a Japanese businessman seeming to say yes to one of our requests and not realizing he may actually mean no but is culturally prevented from using that term in a friendly discussion, we could get into big trouble.

Staying with the language example, at the higher levels of language use, we would not want people to speak or write exactly alike any more than we would want William Faulkner, James Joyce, Emily Dickinson, Tom Wolfe, Hunter S. Thompson, or William Shakespeare to sound alike. We can even come to appreciate the different language inventions in which words sometimes take on meanings precisely the opposite of their conventional definitions. As I have learned from my skateboarding sons, not only does "bad" sometimes mean "good," but "sick" can mean "great." So language is only testable at the simplest and perhaps least interesting levels. Testing and grading at that level sends what some would regard as a rather limiting message about the use of language.

How about learning an athletic skill—say, learning to serve in tennis? Surely that is a skill that can be learned from a teacher or coach. The best players seem to do it the same way. But wait a minute. They don't do it the same way. Everyone develops a slightly different serve to accommodate their physical abilities, the racquet they use, the court surface, or their style of play. Moreover, each time they serve, the serve is further differentiated, informed by an educated response to the situation, a spontaneous reading of their opponent's ability, position on the court, strategy, mood, state of exhaustion, weakness, spirit, momentum or lack of it, and on and on. Any number of other dimensions are unconsciously called into play at that moment, including determining where to place the ball in the serving court, what kind of speed or spin to put on it, and what to communicate by it. Many of these are invented by the player, not the coach. So can we test the skill? Yes, but not in its most important dimensions, its finer points. In the end, it's all about the finer points. For a pro, it is learned as education, not skill. I'm sure the same subtleties, complexities, and individual differences apply to quarterbacking, boxing, pitching, auto racing ... and design.

Acting is also considered a skill and usually taught that way. And it surely is a skill. To appreciate the power of that skilled craft, one only need watch the scene in the film *The French Lieutenant's Woman* in which Meryl Streep plays a scene without acting and then replays it employing acting skills. Yet no acting coach would settle for just a

4V9O9E001EW4

The Power of Design: A Force for Transforming Everything

Aisle 2 Bay 4 Shelf 7   Item 286

Thank you for buying from **Goodwill Big Bend Ind.** on Amazon Marketplace.

Ship To
Thomas Peters
90 ALLEN NECK RD
SOUTH DARTMOUTH, MA 02748-1002

Order Details
Order ID   114-6841811-4189012
Order Date   9/26/2023 8:52:15 AM
Shipping Service   Standard
Buyers Name   thomas j peters

SKU / Listing ID	Title / Condition	Location / Comments
4V9O9E001EW4	The Power of Design: A Force for Transforming	Aisle 2 - Bay 4 - Shelf 7 - Item 286
8547225916161	Everything	
	Acceptable	The dust jacket shows normal wear and tear. There is

Price: $18.73   Shipping: $3.99

some corner dings. This book is in ACCEPTABLE
condition. Book has visible wear. Pages are still intact but
spine may have minor creasing. While in readable
condition we do not recommend gifting this item. No
guarantee discs or access codes are included. Ship to you
from Goodwill- Big Bend Industries.
Code: 9780978555283
ASIN: 0978555287

Goodwill Big Bend Ind. strives to have each and every customer 100% satisfied with their purchase. If for any reason you are not 100% satisfied please email us at ebooks@goodwillbigbend.com with your concerns.

If we need to make something right, we will, <u>Guaranteed!</u>

Thanks for buying on Amazon Marketplace.

skilled actor, wanting instead the actor to merge personal experience and deep feeling into the scripted role and display a broad understanding of the period in history, the writer's intention, the social and cultural context of the drama, the dynamics of the relationships, the nature of playwriting, and so on, all the while inventing and going beyond previous limits on performance and beyond the coach. Is that skill training or education? Is it testable? Impossible.

I am continually impressed by the attitude of many young rock musicians who take pride in not knowing and never intending to learn how to read music. It is estimated that half of all rock musicians, including those at the top, do not read music. Famous stars like pianist Erroll Garner, drummer Buddy Rich, and guitarists Wes Montgomery and Jimi Hendrix never learned to read music. Trumpet idol Chet Baker did not understand the chord structure of music. Famed pianist Dave Brubeck actually graduated from college as a music major without the ability to read music. Legendary jazz trumpeter Louis Armstrong, when questioned as to whether he could read music, answered, "Not enough to hurt my playing." Even the great classical tenor Luciano Pavarotti could not read music. The list of top musicians without such skills is long, but it is significant to note for this discussion that many stars sought to learn music reading skills only after becoming accomplished professionals.

What about reading? Surely that is a skill—learning the alphabet, recognizing words, pronouncing the syllables. We can test for accuracy, speed, comprehension. New methods for teaching the skill are frequently introduced. But we face a curious phenomenon. For most American students, the more they are made to acquire the skill, the less they desire to read. As a consequence, after 13 years of full-time study, of the 71 percent of students who still remain to graduate, it is nothing short of astounding that about half are functionally illiterate. It is not much of an exaggeration to say that in school students learn *not* to read.

Some hold that reading is a skill that, under optimal conditions, takes only a few weeks to learn. What's going on here? I suggest that we are approaching the subject of reading as a skill training exercise when it is really a matter for broader education. Measurement of the skill may only get in the way. The larger interests and potential of the individual student should be looked to before any emphasis is placed on skill development.

In a sense, we may have had it backwards all along. Perhaps skills are not basic after all. Learning skills does not necessarily lead to more advanced interests, but more advanced interests may lead to learning skills.

We can make a similar case for writing, mathematics, computer skills, drawing, and, I would guess, all of the elements of a design curriculum, perhaps showing that there really is no subject that is purely a matter of skill development. Perhaps it is all education, and evaluation is everywhere inappropriate.

Achieving Breakthroughs

Whe not only want students to be different from each other but different from their teachers. What? Don't we want them to learn what the teacher has to teach? Well, yes, but not exactly. Ideally, we want students to transcend the teacher, to go further with some ideas and to creatively set a different course. The best teachers have always fostered that. How can we possibly measure that or even know that it is happening?

Indeed, we know from history that breakthrough ideas, paradigm-changing ideas, sometimes coming from students such as Albert Einstein, are first met with ridicule, then hostility, then grudging acceptance. We don't need to go back to Freud or Darwin or Galileo to find those reactions. When Frederick Smith, as a student, submitted his design and business plan for Federal Express, his professor handed it back with a C grade, advising him that he needed to present something realistic. I am similarly amused as well as disturbed that Maya Lin received a B for her design of the Vietnam Veterans' Memorial. Both of these evaluative sins were committed at Yale, one of America's top institutions of learning. Think what goes on in lesser institutions. In its upper reaches, certainly, educational achievement is totally beyond conventional evaluation.

Evaluating education is complicated by other factors as well. Take timing, for example. Evaluations are typically administered right after a lesson is delivered or at the end of the week or end of a semester. But when is a lesson learned? A lesson may have been highly effective, but the effect may be dormant for years. I still occasionally find myself awaking to the implications of certain ideas I first encountered in graduate school. At the time I never could have convinced any professor that I fully grasped those concepts. Sometimes it takes an event later in life to trigger the learning—the *Oh, now I get it! So that's what he was talking about!* phenomenon. Was it poor teaching? Not in the least. It was highly effective and deeply imprinted. But the student couldn't have passed the test.

So far, I have been pointing to fairly obvious problems with evaluations that the reader may have encountered often before. But there are other, more difficult, paradoxical issues. For example, take the paradoxical idea offered by renowned physicist Niels Bohr that *the opposite of a profound truth is also true*. Architect Ludwig Mies van der Rohe's famous truth, "Less is more" is surely profound. But less is also less. Or this one: "Beauty is in the eye of the beholder." Was there ever a more profound truth? But beauty is also in the object. If a profound truth (and presumably that is what we teachers want to convey) is often true in its opposite, then how do we evaluate a student who expresses the opposite, especially when the student may be expressing the more unconventional of the two. Suppose a student, responding to a test question, were to be the first to articulate the statement, "Beauty is in the eye of the beholder." That jarring truth would not be considered a correct answer. How do we evaluate a student when the answer is more profound than the question? Embarrassing as that may be, isn't it exactly what we would love to happen with our students?

Often the learning is not represented in the curriculum at all but in the interstices between elements or ideas or hidden somewhere in a seemingly idle remark. It may be true that most of our significant learning comes not directly from teachers but from deep within ourselves as some situation we encounter enables us to formulate an idea that we didn't know resided in us. That is why I prefer to address an audience from notes rather than reading a prepared text—I may say something I didn't know that I knew.

With evaluation being such a fundamental part of the education system, failure is measured, graded, and penalized. If failure were seen rather as a necessary step toward success, which is the way it is viewed in the high-tech industries most dependent on innovation, it would not lead to the punishment and embarrassment of getting a bad grade, having to repeat a class or a test, or dropping out. Failure in those innovative industries is not judged but analyzed, becoming the basis for learning and further experimentation. But failure in school is humiliating at best and severely damaging at worst. While not all failure is well-intended or benign, it all has meaning and relevance that deserves understanding.

In recent decades the evaluative emphasis has been placed on what psychologists call positive reinforcement—rewarding the desired behavior. However, extrinsic rewards are counterproductive because students learn to work for the reward rather than the learning, and they quit when the reward is achieved. Extrinsic rewards tend not to have the power of intrinsic rewards that come from accomplishing the work itself.

To show how we must regard failure in school and in the educational system as a whole, perhaps we can use an analogy with the criminal justice system. When we decriminalize a crime, say, drug use or prostitution, we immediately take the worst punishment away. It is no longer cause for arrest and prison. Going a step further, if we legitimize that previously criminal behavior, we are actually accommodating it, finding ways to treat it, but still not condoning it. With failure, we have to go even further. We have to welcome it, embrace it, use it, study and analyze it, build on it ... remove the stigma entirely.

We need to treat success and failure similarly, neither rewarding one nor punishing the other. Better that we treat them nonjudgmentally, with genuine engagement.

Incorporating failure as a plus, not a minus, is therefore a rather intimidating prospect, even if educators were convinced that evaluation is not necessary. Obviously that conviction, that motivation, if it exists, has not been sufficient because evaluation and grading have come under severe criticism for generations without ensuing change. I cannot help but think that if we genuinely believed it is poisonous, ruining lives, we would take action. Well, it is poisonous. It does ruin lives.

None of us wants a system that homogenizes people, loses some of the best teachers and students, casts off deviant or failing members, but that is what we have. It is the direct consequence of standards, evaluation, and risk aversion, and it is dangerous for our civilization for us to continue this way. We need organizations that help create people who can take our society to places we have never dreamed. It has been an entire century since we have produced people who have contributed truly civilization-changing ideas—people like Freud, Einstein, Darwin, Edison, and Gandhi. We need for some of our students to leap ahead of all of us. We need to develop a system that not only permits but encourages it. Not with honors and awards but with the freedom and encouragement that come from nonjudgmental interest.

We are not paralyzed, in any case. The acceptance of failure can play a major role in improving education even without any change in current systems of grading students. Teachers, administrators, and school board members can encourage more risk-taking within the organization and offer support and genuine engagement when failure occurs. That attitude can become contagious. It is happening in business organizations all over the world.

Democracy will always be messy, and partisan politics will always play a role even though evaluation per se is not a partisan issue. Will we encounter strong resistance, argument, outrage? Of course. Will we become frustrated and discouraged? Surely. Can the educational system continue as it is? Probably. It has for centuries. Can we do better? Unquestionably. Much better. But only by failing more.

Part VII
Design in the Public Interest

T his is what it's all about. It's come down to what designers have done and are doing that we could consider metadesign. We will consider the most unfortunate gap between design and the social sciences, what might be done about it, and the current applications of design in the public interest. We'll look at some possibilities for future social design projects. Finally, we will call for an action program to provide a guiding brain trust for the entire field of design.

Given that this part looks to the future of metadesign, I think it appropriate for me to acknowledge that trying to establish what that future holds is more than a bit problematic. The future is notoriously unpredictable. Besides, we have it all wrong. We think that because the future hasn't happened we can do something about it. Actually, we have much more control over the past than we do over the future. It's much easier to rewrite history than to affect what's about to happen. Just kidding, but not entirely.

The late and highly respected futurist Herman Kahn stunned the experts 40 years ago by accurately predicting that Japan, the country we then relied on only for cheap Christmas tree ornaments, was about to become a major global economic power. But in private he confessed to me that in making predictions he had been wrong about almost everything. And he was our best.

Moving Mountains

More than four decades ago, the young social psychologist Robert Sommer noted that the patients of a psychiatric hospital in which he worked sat silently on benches facing each other across a wide hallway. He decided to redesign the area into what looked more like a sidewalk café, with small tables and chairs so that the patients sat at right angles to each other, a more conversational arrangement. The behavior change was dramatic. His now classic studies showed that the increased interaction proved highly beneficial. He had engineered a design solution. He went on to design many more and is now Distinguished Professor of Psychology Emeritus at the University of California at Davis.

After a long period of isolation from this and many hundreds of studies that followed, it is long past time for the field of design to become aware of the existence of a major area of unrealized potential. If designers do come to share this awareness in great numbers, there appears to be no limit to the positive role they can play in the future of our civilization.

As social psychologist and human ecology professor Franklin Becker of Cornell University, who was Robert Sommer's first doctoral student, makes clear in an article in InformeDesign's newsletter, the gap between social science research and design practice remains huge, apparently because the social scientist's interest in evidence-based design leads designers to fear that their creativity may be stifled. Social scientists and designers can work together to overcome that problem and close the gap because it is abundantly clear that designers can make a significant difference in how people live on this planet. Design has tremendous power. As James Cramer, former CEO of the AIA says, "Design can move mountains."

All right, let's move those mountains. What is it going to take? First of all, let's look at the effort in this direction that has already taken place, and that is a considerable amount. Work has been going on for several decades in environmental psychology, as evidenced by the existence of such research journals as *Environment and Behavior*, the *Journal of Architectural and Planning Research*, and the *Journal of Environmental Psychology*. The Environmental Design Research Association has existed since the 1960s. Some designers have long struggled to live professional lives closer to their higher callings. For example, the Design Manifesto was created by a group of top graphic designers and published by the American Institute of Graphic Arts:

> "We, the undersigned, are graphic designers, art directors and visual communicators who have been raised in a world in which the techniques and apparatus of advertising have persistently been presented to us as the most lucrative, effective and desirable use of our talents. Many design teachers and mentors promote this belief; the market rewards it; a tide of books and publications reinforces it.
>
> "Encouraged in this direction, designers then apply their skill and imagination to sell dog biscuits, designer coffee, diamonds, detergents, hair gel, cigarettes, credit cards, sneakers, butt toners, light beer and heavy-duty recreational vehicles. Commercial work has always paid the bills, but many graphic designers have now let it become, in large measure, what graphic designers do. This, in turn, is how the world perceives design. The profession's time and energy is used up manufacturing demand for things that are inessential at best.
>
> "Many of us have grown increasingly uncomfortable with this view of design. Designers who devote their efforts primarily to advertising, marketing and brand development are supporting, and implicitly endorsing, a mental environment so saturated with commercial messages that it is changing the very way citizen-consumers speak,

think, feel, respond and interact. To some extent we are all helping draft a reductive and immeasurably harmful code of public discourse.

"There are pursuits more worthy of our problem-solving skills. Unprecedented environmental, social and cultural crises demand our attention. Many cultural interventions, social marketing campaigns, books, magazines, exhibitions, educational tools, television programs, films, charitable causes and other information design projects urgently require our expertise and help.

"We propose a reversal of priorities in favor of more useful, lasting and democratic forms of communication—a mindshift away from product marketing and toward the exploration and production of a new kind of meaning. The scope of debate is shrinking; it must expand. Consumerism is running uncontested; it must be challenged by other perspectives expressed, in part, through the visual languages and resources of design.

"In 1964, 22 visual communicators signed the original call for our skills to be put to worthwhile use. With the explosive growth of global commercial culture, their message has only grown more urgent. Today, we renew their manifesto in expectation that no more decades will pass before it is taken to heart."

Many graphic designers, including some of the most distinguished, signed this renewal of the manifesto. It is but one of a number of efforts to bring a new consciousness of the role of designer in our society. Some efforts, such as those mentioned in the following pages, are giving designers new assistance and new outlets for the expression of their talents toward a higher calling.

InformeDesign, a collaboration between the University of Minnesota and the American Society of Interior Designers, has developed and now houses in extensive archives a most valuable and searchable database of summaries of design and human behavior research projects. It also produces a monthly newsletter devoted to building bridges between design and environmental and social science research.

Public Architecture, operating out of San Francisco, puts the resources of architecture in the service of the public interest. The group identifies and solves practical problems of human interaction in the built environment and acts as a catalyst for public discourse through education, advocacy, and the design of public spaces and amenities. One major program is The 1 Percent Solution, which enlists design firms in a commitment to devote 1 percent of their time and resources to pro bono activities in the public interest.

Architects/Designers/Planners for Social Responsibility is the group I mentioned earlier because of its current and major effort calling for a complete boycott of the building of prisons by these professions.

Habitat for Humanity is perhaps the best known such organization. It is a nonprofit, ecumenical Christian housing organization building simple, affordable housing in partnership with people in need. Its most famous leader is President Jimmy Carter, and it has already housed a million needy people in 225,000 homes worldwide.

Architecture for Humanity also works all over the globe, providing a range of services to community groups, nongovernmental organizations, and others seeking architecture and design services. In addition, through its design fellowship program and financial sponsorship, it provides support to designers who offer pro bono services to community groups. It has helped people displaced by Hurricane Katrina in New Orleans, helped with reconstruction after the Sumatra tsunami, and helped with the development of a rural health center in Tanzania, the first in Africa.

Seawater Foundation transforms desert coastlines into fertile growing areas by irrigating with seawater. Designed by Carl Hodges, director emeritus of the Environmental Research Laboratory at the University of Arizona, this process enables the growing of edible halophyte crops fertilized by effluent from shrimp farms that also create forests of mangrove trees, which supply lumber and restore carbon into the soil, all the while keeping the seawater on the beaches clear and clean. Besides this remarkable green environmental design, it permits the development of communities along these previously poverty stricken areas that can support themselves by making or harvesting products from the various seawater-nourished crops.

Design that Matters creates new products that allow social enterprises in developing countries to offer improved services and scale more quickly. Design that Matters has built a collaborative design process through which hundreds of volunteers in academia and industry donate their skills and expertise to the creation of breakthrough products for communities in need. Design that Matters has worked with indigenous groups, the disabled, and the elderly. Student teams have tackled such challenges as a nonelectric incubator for premature infants in rural areas, a children's talking toy for American Indian language preservation, and a "smart" cane for the blind.

These organizations illustrate the ability of the design professions to address metadesign issues. The challenge is to increase the scale of their activity a thousandfold and to enter areas that even they have not yet ventured into.

Let me suggest a few projects that have particularly interested me. I most want to eradicate slums, overcome diseases, reduce the suffering of poverty. But I also hope designers will address some additional possibilities that grow out of work they or some social scientists have already accomplished.

For example, we know that being exposed to nature is simply good for us. And that exposure does not need to entail surfing big waves or running in open fields. It turns out that when two young boys both live in a housing project, one looking out the window at greenery and the other at a cement wall, the one looking at greenery will do better in school and be less likely to get into trouble with the law. Similarly, a surgery patient in a hospital room that has a view of nature will recover much faster than a patient without a view. In meeting rooms with windows, people are smarter. The list goes on.

Other studies make me want to know if designers could work together across disciplines and with social scientists to develop designs that would encourage families to engage in activities leading to less family dysfunction and healthy outcomes for children. We know that designers could reduce crime, if only by refraining from building giant prisons and instead keep the convicts in smaller groups of about 18. But there are surely other things they might do to reduce crime, such as perhaps reducing domestic violence and child abuse. We know that child abuse is committed almost entirely by parents, at least hundreds of thousands of times a year and perhaps much more frequently. For example, David Gil, author of Violence Against Children, estimates perhaps 4.2 million occasions a year. Most of these frantic parents are frustrated by the increasingly burdensome parenting role. Can we design to make that role less difficult and lonely? Can we reverse the current trend of making parents afraid of strangers, and make strangers available to help?

We know that the single best protection against both mental and physical illness is being in a relationship, even if it is with an animal. That is one reason why being in a community is so good for us. Community means that we often accidentally encounter people with whom we are acquainted and even have helpful relations occasionally with people in the community whom we don't know. Not everyone understands just how important community is. If they did, they would never allow the erosion of community that has taken place in the past few decades. That erosion comes mainly from the development of shopping centers and in particular the big box stores like Wal-Mart and discount houses like Costco. Prices are significantly lower in such places, but it is a false economy. It isn't just that we need to buy second cars to get to those places. It's that they force out of business the local merchants that have operated the grocery stores, hardware stores, book stores, drug stores, and liquor stores where we used to run into our friends. We think that by buying a bottle of whiskey for $3 less than we would pay at our local liquor store we are saving money. But we know that the loss of community results in an increase in crime and illness, and I suspect that it also contributes to an increase in divorce, addiction, child abuse, suicide—all immensely costly.

Moreover, we lose the services that create the feelings of connection that make us feel more human. The person staffing the liquor store is someone we get to know. He recognizes us. We converse. He will ask about our family, cash our check, give us advice about which wine we might want to buy. And before the competition from those discount houses forced the local liquor store into near bankruptcy, he would offer more services, deliver what we purchased, help us plan a gathering, furnish the glasses and the ice, making our staging of such gatherings of friends more likely. Most important, he knows who we are, and if something were to happen to us he would know whom to call. That is community, and we are losing it fast. But we can influence changes. Again, much of it is to refrain from doing the things that erode it— housing projects with no center, no shared facilities, no connections with others. We have yet to see a boycotting of shopping centers, but who knows? I would love to see an interdisciplinary team work on the issue of creating community, knowing that large-scale public funding would be possible.

The best city planners find most of their dreams still on the drawing boards, unable to implement them because as a society we have never been able to mobilize the community support for them. So we are not only ill-prepared for massive evacuations and other constructive responses to disasters, but as a community we cannot make good decisions about those plans or even know about them and understand them. But we can be helped by designers willing to make use of the fact that there are several very expensive pieces of terminal equipment in practically every home in America—television, telephone, radio, newspaper, computer, and more and more high-technology games, cell phones, personal digital assistants, and the like. These instruments have never been linked as a mechanism to simulate a major problem such as an environmental disaster, a terror attack, or a riot, each presented in a graphically powerful way, followed by various responsive scenarios that could be adopted, rejected, or altered by viewers.

The entire procedure could be local, national, or global, the audience organized into individual or team players in a dramatic simulation exercise, participating in a highly interactive way because of the technology capabilities. Video games are now so sophisticated that they can be shaped and redesigned as they are being used by participants individually or in teams. Any exercise could last for hours or days, involve televised discussion groups, and other groups could be formed in communities and monitored. We could show a compelling scenario about what we would be up against as a society so that we could have a chance to experience, in our guts, the magnitude of the problem and come to better responses. We are sadly unprepared for any such tragic events, and I think it is foolish not to use the multibillions of dollars' worth of already existing terminal technology to help us design a better society for ourselves.

In that regard, we could use the same participative simulation and gaming design to improve our education, our democracy, our voting, our health. There is no end of positive uses. But we must realize that this kind of an event does not lend itself to commercial television and would in all likelihood have to be organized and presented by public broadcasting and almost surely need to be funded by the public or nonprofit sector.

I would like to close this chapter with another word from Tom Fisher, whom you may remember I quoted in the introduction of this book. He is dean of the College of Design at the University of Minnesota and former editor of Progressive Architecture. These were his final words in the same article after commenting on the need for metadesign, its similarity to public health, and the probability of funding in billions from the World Bank and the World Health Organization:

"Largely missing are the architects able to help find creative design solutions and ensure efficient delivery of human habitation, and prepared to work as ... 'metadesigners,' assembling and coordinating the complex teams necessary to address the enormity of the problem. It's a calling we can no longer ignore."

31
Getting Serious About the Future

Metadesign escalates in both scale and scope all of the areas of design. It can become involved in the large-scale issues of slum eradication, voting design, and disaster response, as well as the most personal and intimate aspects of family life, reducing divorce, child abuse, and mental illness. There are many barriers to its accomplishment, much to think through. And the need for continuous attention, response, and direction will be with us for the foreseeable future.

When I was on the Board of Directors of the AIA, I felt the need for a think tank that could address the higher-order issues that our board could not. I suspect that all design professional societies' boards have the same problem—not enough time to discuss the issues of metadesign and probably not the right makeup of the group to do so.

It is impossible to overestimate the importance of design, yet there is no high-level forum, no group of eminent leaders devoted solely to thinking about the future of design, creating alternative scenarios, addressing the fundamental and long-range issues. Indeed, architecture and design can be said to suffer from a lack of attention from such a distinguished body. Professional societies, having to devote most of their time and resources to dealing with issues of pressing current importance, seldom have the opportunity to consider the longer-range possibilities.

I would like to see the development of a think tank devoted to long-term strategies that could serve all of the design professions, help with the link to the social sciences, end the internecine warfare among designers, and focus on the future of design. This prestigious and continuing international forum could be composed of eminent leaders drawn from many fields, in rotating membership—the wisest, most experienced, open-minded and outstanding leaders in each of the design professions, of course, but also including distinguished scientists, artists, academics, public intellectuals, former government officials, university presidents, and top CEOs—to examine the role of design in building a better world.

They would analyze the global needs for design intervention, the potential contribution design professions can make to meet those needs, the changing economic and social context in which design professions operate, the relevant scientific and technological advances that could shape new methods of design, the new media that could extend the reach and power of the design professions, and creative approaches to overcoming barriers to change, particularly the barriers to large-scale public funding. The wisdom of these top leaders would be communicated to the professions, to policymakers, and to the general public. Their deliberations would be constantly guided by the intent to bring about the policies and practices necessary to take the professions of design to new heights of achievement.

In writing this book, I ran across the transcript of the 1975 keynote address at the International Design Conference in Aspen, with the theme The Right to a Well Designed World, given by Harlan Cleveland, former ambassador to NATO and president of the University of Hawaii. I was impressed by how important even then he thought such a body might be. His words:

> "To match the macro problems we face together, we need to build an international consortium of the concerned, a community of continuous consultation about the human purposes our imaginative designs and our miraculous technologies are going to serve.
>
> "If we miss this chance, here or soon, we who presume to design the future and are called leaders in our own neighborhoods will deserve that devastatingly snide comment of Girardoux: 'The privilege of the great is to watch catastrophe from a terrace.'"

Acknowledgements

I n preparing this manuscript, I incorporated adaptations of several articles I previously published in *Domus, DesignIntelligence, Perspectives, arcCA*, as well as parts of a chapter in my book *Birthrights: A Bill of Rights for Children*, and parts of a chapter in *Engaging Every Learner*, edited by Alan M.Blankstein, Robert W. Cole, and Paul D. Houston. I am further indebted to family and friends, to my colleagues in various design and social science groups to which I have belonged and from whom I learned so much. I am particularly grateful to my WBSI colleagues Rosemary Ennis, Andrea Lawrence-Stuart, and Kip Winsett for their help, accommodation, and encouragement, and to my editor, Jane Gaboury, for her wisdom and unstinting devotion to this project. Finally, I probably would not have written this book without the confidence and urging of Design Futures Council President and Co-chair James Cramer. Thanks to all of you.

About the Author

Richard Farson, Ph.D., is a psychologist, author, and educator. As co-founder and president of the Western Behavioral Sciences Institute, he directs the Institute's centerpiece program, the International Leadership Forum, a think tank of influential leaders addressing the critical policy issues of our time. Long interested in the field of design, Farson was founding dean of the School of Design at the California Institute of the Arts and a 30-year member of the Board of Directors of the International Design Conference in Aspen, of which he was president for seven years. He served on the American Institute of Architects Board of Directors and is a Senior Fellow of the Design Futures Council. His most recent books include *Management of the Absurd: Paradoxes in Leadership*, and *Whoever Makes the Most Mistakes Wins: The Paradox of Innovation* (with co-author Ralph Keyes).

Also from Greenway and Östberg

Almanac of Architecture & Design
James P. Cramer and Jennifer Evans Yankopolus, editors

For years, the *Almanac of Architecture & Design* has annually provided readers with sweeping views of events, benchmarks, and successes of the previous year in design. Included are essential lists of award winners, design leaders, building types, records, rankings, organizations, and resources.

America's Best Architecture & Design Schools

The nation's leading survey to evaluate programs based on the satisfaction of the professionals who do the hiring, this annual issue ranks architecture, landscape architecture, interior design, and industrial design programs. Hiring managers from top firms evaluate recent graduates for practice readiness in a range of skills.

Architecture and the Brain:
A New Knowledge Base from Neuroscience
John P. Eberhard

A stimulant to architects, the neuroscience community, and the general reader, this book can serve as the base for exploratory studies on the interface between architectural settings and human experiences and provide insight into issues not previously contemplated.

Business Comes to the Expert:
A Proactive Marketing Plan for Professional Practice Firms
Brenda Richards and Kathleen Soldati

Go beyond reactively answering requests for proposals and position your firm as a sought-after provider of professional services. Readers will find not only new ways of thinking about marketing, but they'll also get the strategies and tools they need to put these concepts into practice.

Change Design:
Conversations About Architecture as the Ultimate Business Tool
NBBJ and Bruce Mau

A quiet revolution is underway. There's a growing awareness that innovation is critical to business competitiveness and that design is critical to innovation. *Change Design* explores how a new approach that integrates design with business performance will replace traditional form-driven architecture.

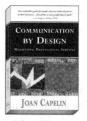

Communication by Design: Marketing Professional Services
Joan Capelin

How to communicate—and, especially why—to clients, prospects, staff, and the public is the basis of *Communication by Design*. It is targeted to professional practice principals as well as anyone who aspires to a leadership position in a firm, association, or strategic alliance.

Compensation and Salary Survey

This must-have annual reference includes current salary and bonus levels for intern architects, architects, project managers, interior designers, landscape architects, engineers, marketing staff, specialty and support staff, principals, partners, and C-titles. Included are salary projections as well as data about benefits, perks, and strategic practices.

Design Plus Enterprise:
Seeking a New Reality in Architecture & Design
James P. Cramer

This is a classic on vision for professional practices. Arthur Gensler calls it "must-reading for every architect." Using specific examples, *Design Plus Enterprise* illustrates how architects can create better design services—and thereby a better society—by using business principles. It also demonstrates how smart design can drive economic success.

DesignIntelligence Subscription

DesignIntelligence is the Design Futures Council's bi-monthly report on the future and the repository of a wealth of timely articles, authoritative research, and trends reports. Along with original articles by legendary names in the AEC field, *DesignIntelligence* offers groundbreaking insight on future trends and management practices.

How Firms Succeed: A Field Guide to Design Management
James P. Cramer and Scott Simpson

Use this hands-on guide to run any design-related business—from a two-person graphics team to mid-sized and global firms. The authors combine practical solutions with business theory, providing insight into the art of inspirational management and strategic thinking.

Leadership by Design: Creating an Architecture of Trust
Richard N. Swett

Ambassador Swett's groundbreaking book investigates the unique civic leadership strengths of the architecture profession. It is an eloquent plea to architects, leaders, and citizens alike to seek new leadership to design solutions for the complex challenges facing our nation and the world.

The Next Architect: A New Twist on the Future of Design
James P. Cramer and Scott Simpson

This national bestseller shows how tomorrow's successful practitioners will be adept at collaborative design techniques and comfortable working at warp speed. *The Next Architect* challenges the next generation of design professionals to make full use of their talents to build a better, healthier, and more prosperous world.

Reach Higher: Long-cycle Strategies for a Short-cycle World
Ed Friedrichs

Using a very personal leadership journey through a highly acclaimed career, Ed Friedrichs makes the case for a quantum shift in thinking about organizational design in the new business environment where people resources, embedded knowledge, culture, and trust relationships are an enterprise's most strategic valuable assets.

Value Redesigned: New Models for Professional Practice
Kyle V. Davy and Susan L. Harris

Architects and engineers can be pre-eminent value creators, and this book presents an in-depth look into that potential future. It explores the adaptive challenges firms face as they move into the future and offers guidance for the difficult transformational work required for genuine success.

Find more titles and ordering information at
www.greenway.us/bookstore or (800) 726-8603

östberg™

Library of Design Management

Every relationship of value requires constant care and commitment. At Östberg, we are relentless in our desire to create and bring forward only the best ideas in design, architecture, interiors, and design management. Using diverse mediums of communications, including books and the Internet, we are constantly searching for thoughtful ideas that are erudite, witty, and of lasting importance to the quality of life. Inspired by the architecture of Ragnar Östberg and the best of Scandinavian design and civility, the Östberg Library of Design Management seeks to restore the passion for creativity that makes better products, spaces, and communities. The essence of Östberg can be summed up in our quality character to you: "Communicating concepts of leadership and design excellence."